# A TOUR IN WALES

# A Tour in Wales
## by Thomas Pennant

### ABRIDGED BY DAVID KIRK

GWASG Carreg Gwalch

ISBN: 0-86381-473-5

Cover design: Alan Jones

First published in 1998 by Gwasg Carreg Gwalch,
12 Iard yr Orsaf, Llanrwst, Wales LL26 0EH
☎ (01492) 642031
Printed and published in Wales

# Author's Introduction

AMONG THE gentleman I am chiefly indebted to for information respecting the present work, I cannot pass unthanked Philip Yorke of Erddig, John Mytton of Halston, Thomas Mostyn of the house of Trelacre, Peter Davies of Broughton, Kenrick Eyton of Eyton, Paul Panton of Bagillt, Lloyd Kenyon of Gredington and Roger Kenyon of Cefn.

To the late Richard Morris of the navy office I owed much general information. Mr Hawker of the customs house, Chester, favoured me with a particular account of the commerce of that city. The reverend Mr Edwards, rector of Llanfechan, favoured me with some excellent accounts of the parishes of Oswestry, Selattyn and Hope.

I received several historical facts respecting the parish of Whittington from the reverend Mr Roberts, rector of the parish. The reverend Mr John Price, public librarian, and the reverend Mr John Jones, fellow of Jesus college, Oxford, were indefatigable in furnishing me with extracts from the manuscripts of the university.

As due, I must repeat my thanks to the reverend Mr John Lloyd, rector of Caerwys, and late of Nannerch, my constant companion in these excursions, for variety of information which his great knowledge of our ancient language qualified him to give, to my singular advantage.

Mr Wilkinson, painter in Chester, obliged me with many materials relative to that city. My thanks also to Mr Calvely, land surveyor of the same city, and to the reverend Mr Richard Williams of Fron.

The drawings marked Moses Griffith are the performances of a worthy servant whom I keep for that purposes. The candid will excuse any little imperfections they may find in them as they are the works of an untaught genius drawn from the most remote and obscure parts of North Wales.

**Thomas Pennant, February 1st 1778**

# Editor's Introduction

**THOMAS PENNANT** was born on June 14th 1726 at Whitford near the town of Trefynnon in what is now the county of Clwyd. He was the eldest son of David Pennant who inherited the family home, Downing, from a distant relative two years before Thomas' birth. The Pennant family traced its descent from Madog ap Meilor who settled in the parish during the 12th century after marrying the heiress of Bychton, an estate adjoining Downing. Madog was in turn descended from Twdor Trefor an his wife Angharad, the daughter of Hywel Dda. The family surname derives from Bychton's location at the *head* (pen) of a *valley* (nant). Thomas appears to have been given his first-name in memory of David Pennant's benefactor.

Little can be learnt of Pennant's early life from his own writings. He suffered during childhood a mild attack of smallpox which became severe through unskilful treatment. A sustained interest in natural history began when, at the age of 12, he was given a copy of Francis Willughby's *Ornithology*. Educated in Wrecsam and later in London, Pennant entered Oxford University in March 1744. Two years into his Oxford studies, Pennant travelled to Cornwall where he developed a friendship with the Cornish antiquary and naturalist William Borlase who encouraged him in the study of minerology and history. Pennant left Oxford without graduating but, as the heir of a wealthy father, had no immediate need to earn a living. He continued his studies, contributing occasional articles to the *Philosophical Transactions of the Royal Society* . His first printed work was a description of an earthquake which shook Downing in April 1750. He became a Fellow of the Society of Antiquarians in 1754 and toured Ireland that same year, evidently enjoying the country but leaving no written account. In 1755 he began a long correspondence with the Swedish botanist Carl Linnaeus and was elected a member of the Royal Society of Upsala.

In 1759, Pennant married Elizabeth, daughter of James Falconer of Chester, and settled at Whitford. There he commenced his first book, *British Zoology*, which resulted in his election as a Fellow of the Royal Society. David Pennant died in 1763, leaving Thomas and Elizabeth in possession of Downing but any pleasure brought by this inheritance was offset by Elizabeth's death just one year later. Perhaps to divert his thoughts, Pennant travelled through Europe in 1765, visiting the naturalist Georges Buffon and the writer Voltaire in France, Baron Haller in Bern and the Dutch naturalist Pallas. His interest in mining and minerals found practical application in identifying and exploiting a rich vein of lead at Downing. The profits from this venture allowed substantial improvements to the house and estate. His description of the house conveys as much about the author as about the building:

'The house itself has little to boast of. I fortunately found it incapable of being improved into a magnitude exceeding the revenue of the family. It has a hall, which I prefer to the rural impropriety of a paltry vestibule; a library; a parlour capable of containing more guests than I ever wish to see at one time, and a smoking-room most antiquely furnished with ancient carvings and the horns of all the European beasts of chase. This room is now quite out of use as to its original purpose. Above stairs is a good drawing-room, in times of old called the dining-room, and a tea-room, the sum of all that are really wanted. I have Cowley's wish realised: a small house and a large garden!'

*British Zoology* was followed by supplemental volumes and a *History of British Quadrupeds*. In 1769, Pennant travelled through Scotland and compiled detailed notes which formed the basis of a *Tour in Scotland*. This journey appears to have been made primarily to study Scottish plants and animals but the book demonstrates Pennant's interest in humanity which became the most rewarding feature of his subsequent tours.

Pennant was accompanied in Scotland and on later travels by Moses Griffith who combined the functions of manservant and self-taught artist. Griffith was born on April 6th 1749 at Trygain House in the parish of Bryn Groer in the Llŷn peninsular so was 23 years younger than his employer. Pennant encouraged Griffith's study of drawing and engraving and thus solved the problem of illustration which many earlier and later travel writers simply chose to ignore.

The three tours of Wales which form the basis of this volume took place in 1773 and 1776 and were published between 1778 and 1781. A corrected version comprising two volumes followed in 1784 under the title *A Tour in Wales* and it is that edition on which this abridgement is based. Pennant's narrative had evolved from the daily diary style of his earlier tours, further strengthened by an intimate knowledge of the country's history and topography. The result was not merely a classic work in itself but a reference text for several generations of later travel writers, few of whom troubled to acknowledge their source.

After many years as a widower, Pennant married a second time in 1777. His new wife was Ann, the sister of his friend and neighbour Sir Roger Mostyn. The marriage was a very happy one and considerably reduced Pennant's appetite for travelling. He applied himself to new books and to revised editions of his existing works. *Journey from Chester* to London appeared in 1782, followed in 1785 by *Arctic Zoology* and in 1790 by a *History of London* 'composed from the observations of about half a life'. By 1793, at the age of 67, Pennant felt the time had arrived for a concluding autobiography, *The Literary Life of the late Thomas Pennant, by Himself* to announce 'the termination of his authorial existence'. The title reflects the book's content which includes relatively little about his personal activity. Pennant's literary life was in fact anything but terminated. In 1796 he published a *History of Whiteford and Holywell*, one of his best works despite being interrupted by the death of his youngest daughter and of Sir Roger Mostyn.

All Pennant travels were made on horseback, an activity to which he largely attributed the uninterrupted good health of his adulthood. In advancing years, he contented his active mind with armchair travel, planning a series of books under the collective title *Outlines of the Globe* and in 1798 published a two-volume *View of Hindoostan*. Two more volumes (*China, Japan and New Holland* and *The Archipelago of the Indian Ocean*) were completed in manuscript the same year shortly before his death on December 16th at the age of 72. His son David supervised the publication of these works in 1801 along with a *Journey from London to Dover* and *Journey from Dover to the Isle of Wight*.

Moses Griffith remained in the Pennant family's employ for some 50 years, working both for Thomas and David and receiving a pension in retirement. His services were commemorated on his tombstone by David Pennant: "In memory of Moses Griffith, an ingenious self-taught Artist who accompanied Thomas Pennant, the Historian, in his Tours, whose works he illustrated with his faithful Pencil. Died November 11th, 1819, Aged 72."

*A Tour in Wales* is widely recognised as Pennant's finest work. The first of its three parts embraces Chester, Oswestry, Llangollen, Yr Wyddgrug and Caerwys. Part Two covers a much broader area, extending to Dolgellau and Abermaw in the southwest, north again to Betws-y-coed and then through Eryri in magnificent detail to the farthest reaches of Llyn. Thence northwards through Clynnog and Caernarfon into Môn before crossing the Menai to explore Conwy, Llandudno and Rhuddlan. Part Three is a much shorter work, taking author and reader south from Downing as far as Shrewsbury.

Though a competent student of French and Latin, Pennant had a very limited Welsh vocabulary. The children of wealthy families in 18th century Wales were educated in English and thus isolated from the beauty and richness of Welsh literature and culture. Pennant largely overcame this limitation by inviting the reverend John Lloyd of Caerwys to accompany him on each of his tours through Wales. Lloyd assisted both as an interpreter and as an adviser on Welsh history and genealogy. Family ancestries and intermarriages occupy so much space in the original *Tour in Wales* that the text becomes very dry in places except to readers with a specific interest in the ancestry of the larger Welsh estate-holders. This information would have been published partly as a way of thanking the many families Pennant visited during his peregrinations. Being under obligation primarily to Pennant himself, I have therefore taken the liberty of reducing the genealogical diatribes except where of direct historical relevance.

This edition follows the original itineraries exactly, concentrating on social, topographical and geological content. Personal names and place-names have been corrected where necessary, avoiding the corrupted and often inconsistent spellings of the 17th century. Particular care has been taken when editing the second of the three tours (*Journey to Snowdon*) which will be of interest to the widest audience and is certainly the best written. The text of *Journey to Snowdon* in this edition is published almost in full. Readers wishing to follow Pennant's various routes, either at home or in reality, will find the 1:50,000 Ordnance Survey maps of North Wales useful references.

My concluding thanks to Myrddin ap Dafydd of Gwasg Carreg Gwalch for his encouragement and assistance in making possible, for the first time, a compact and widely affordable edition of Thomas Pennant's *A Tour in Wales*.

**David Kirk, February 1998**

# WELSH PLACE NAMES WITH COMMONLY USED ENGLISH VARIANTS

| | |
|---|---|
| Aberffraw | *Aberfraw* |
| Abermaw | *Barmouth* |
| Afon Dyfrdwy | *River Dee* |
| Bangor Is-coed | *Bangor-on-Dee* |
| Biwmares | *Beaumaris* |
| Brycheiniog | *Brecknockshire* |
| Caernarfon | *Caernarvonshire* |
| Ceredigion | *Cardiganshire* |
| Chwitffordd | *Whitford* |
| Dinbych | *Denbighshire* |
| Eryri | *Snowdonia* |
| Estyn | *Hope* |
| Fflint | *Flintshire* |
| Llyn Efyrnwy | *Lake Vyrnwy* |
| Maesyfed | *Radnorshire* |
| Meirionnydd | *Merioneth* |
| Penarlâg | *Hawarden* |
| Porth Dinllaen | *Portin-llaen* |
| Ruthun | *Ruthin* |
| Trefaldwyn | *Montgomery* |
| Treffynnon | *Holywell* |
| Y Waun | *Chirk* |
| Y Trallwng | *Welshpool* |
| Y Fflint | *Flint* |
| Ynys Enlli | *Bardsey* |
| Ynys Môn | *Anglesey* |
| Ynysoedd y Moelrhoniaid | *The Skerries* |
| Yr Wyddgrug | *Mold* |
| Yr Wyddfa | *Snowdon* |

# A Tour in North Wales, 1773

## Chapter One

## Downing to Chester

I NATURALLY begin my journey from the place of my nativity, Downing, in the parish of Whitford in the county of Fflint. This is the least of the Welsh shires. Its northern side is washed by the estuary of the Afon Dyfrdwy, the Seteia Estuarium of Ptolemy. The land rises suddenly from the shore in fine inequalities, clayey and plenteous in corn and grass for 2, 3 or 4 miles, to a mountainous tract that runs parallel to it for a considerable way. The lower parts abound with coal and free-stone; the upper with minerals of lead and calamine, and immense strata of limestone and chert. The principal trade of the country is mining and smelting.

The northern part of Fflint is flat and very rich in corn, especially wheat, which is generally exported to Liverpool. The shire in most places raises more than is sufficient for the use of the inhabitants. It is extremely populous and in the mineral parts composed of a mixed people whose fathers and grandfathers resorted here for employment out of the English mining counties. Many of their children, born of Welsh mothers, have quite lost the language of their fathers.

A lofty range of mountains rises on the west and forms a bold frontier. Our county is watered by several small rivers such as the Alun, the Terrig and the Chwiler; part of its western boundary by the Clwyd; and the Maelor (a disjointed part of the country) by the Dyfrdwy.

When the Roman invaders landed in Britain, northern Wales was possessed by the Ordovices, a name derived from the language of the country bounded by the Afon Dyfrdwy and the Dyfi. The Dyfrdwy flows into the Irish sea below Chester and the Dyfi into the same sea on the borders of Ceredigion. The Ordovices, of which all west of Cheshire was part, had reguli or lords who ruled over little districts and united under a common leader when the exigencies of the time required. These factions weakened the state, separated their interest and facilitated their conquest

*Chester Castle in 1777*

by the first invaders. Gwynedd is the most ancient name we are acquainted with for the land of northern Wales.

The spirit which the people showed at the beginning did not desert them to the last. Though obliged to submit to the resistless power of the Romans, they never fell prey to the enervating charms of luxury as other nations of this island did. The hardy Saxons, for above three centuries, could not make an impression even on our low lands. Offa was the first, extending his kingdom for some miles within our borders. His conquest was but temporary for we repossessed Chester, the capital of the Cornavii, till the year 883 when it was wrested from us by the united force of the Heptarchy beneath the able Egbert. This indeed reduced our confines but did not subdue our spirit. With obdurate valour we sustained our independence for another four centuries against the power of a kingdom more than twelve times larger than Wales, and at length had the glory of falling, when a divided country, beneath the arms of the most wise and most warlike of the English monarchs, Edward I.

Contrary to what happens to most subdued nations, our country preserved its own language and the conquerors even deigned to adopt the names of the Celtic towns and people, latinising them from the original words. Thus London became Londinium from Lundein, derived from Llong Din (or Dinas), the city of ships, from its considerable commerce.

The whole of Fflint was subdued by the Saxons immediately after the taking of Chester by Egbert. It was an open country, destitute of inaccessible rocks and mountains like the rest of northern Wales. The conquerors, as usual, new-named the towns, villages and hamlets but could not cancel the ancient. Thus Hawarden is still known to the Welsh as Penarlâg, Mold as Yr Wyddgrug and Hope as Estyn.

When the Domesday survey was taken, Y Fflint was considered as an appendage of Cheshire by conquest. It is observable that there were only 7 churches at that time in the whole hundred; parochial divisions had not yet taken place. Mr Agard, a writer in the latter end of the 16th century, remarks that the old historians made no mention of either parishes, parsons, vicars, incumbents or curates. The people attended, in those days, either the cathedral churches or the conventual, which were served by the prelates or monks, and those often assisted by presbyters, clerks, and deacons. As piety gained strength, other churches were erected by the nobility and men of property desirous of spiritual assistance within their precincts. The places which enjoyed this advantage had the title Llan prefixed, as that of Tre (a habitation) is to the townships.

Thus in our parish is Tremostyn, remarkable for the ancient seat of

*Maen Achwynfan*

14

the family of the same name. The great gloomy hall is of very old date. The walls are furnished with ancient militia guns, swords and pikes, with helmets and breastplates, with funereal achievements and with variety of spoils of chase. During the time that Henry Tudor was secretly laying the foundation of the overthrow of the house of York, he passed concealed from place to place in order to form an interest among the Welsh who favoured his cause on account of their respect for his grandfather, Owain Tudur, their countryman. While Henry was at Mostyn, a party attached to Richard III arrived there to apprehend him. He was then about to dine but had just time to leap out of a back window and make his escape through a hole which to this day is called the king's. Rhisiart ap Hywel, then Lord of Mostyn, joined Henry at the battle of Bosworth and, after the victory, received from the king, in token of gratitude for his preservation, the belt and sword he wore on the day. Richard was pressed greatly to follow Henry to court but nobly answered "I dwell among mine own people".

Thomas ap Rhisiart ap Hywel ap Ieuan Fychan (Lord of Mostyn) and his brother Piers (founder of the family of Trelacre) were the first who abridged their name and that on the following occasion. Rowland Lee, Bishop of Lichfield and president of the marches of Wales, in the reign of Henry VIII, sat at one of the courts on a Welsh cause and, wearied with the quantity of aps in the jury, directed that the panel should assume their last name or that of their residence, and that Thomas ap Richard ap Hywel ap Ieuan Fychan should for the future be reduced to the poor dissyllable Mostyn, no doubt to the great mortification of many an ancient line.

In the higher part of Mostyn stands the curious cross called Maen Achwynfan, or the stone of lamentation, because penances were often finished before such sacred pillars and concluded with weeping and the usual marks of contrition. I do not presume to attempt to guess at the age though it must have been previous to the reign of gross superstition among the Welsh otherwise the sculptor would have employed his chisel in legendary stories instead of the elegant knots and interlaced work that cover the stone.

A nearby ancient chapel, now a farmhouse called Gelli, was granted by Edward I to the abbot and convent. The abbot was also given the power to grub up the wood which, by the present nakedness of the place, appears to have been done effectually.

From the summit of Garreg, a hill in this parish, the traveller may have an august foresight of the lofty tract of Yr Wyddfa, from the crooked Moel Siabod at one end to the towering Penmaen-mawr at the other, of the vast promontory of Llandudno and part of Ynys Môn; and to the north (at times) the Isle of Man and the Cumberland Alps, the sure presages of bad weather.

The products of Folebroc or Feilebroc are corn of every sort, excepting rye. Little cheese or butter is made here for sale, as the grass is chiefly consumed by horses; for the farmers are greatly employed in carrying the minerals of the country. The same may be said of the shire in general. Every cottager has his potato garden, which is a great support and was a convenience unknown 50 years ago.

The collieries of Mostyn and Bychton have been worked for a very considerable space and in the last century supplied Dublin and the eastern side of Ireland with coals. They were discovered in the township of Mostyn as early as the time of Edward I. They are at present in a low state, partly from the rise of the works at Whitehaven but more from the loss of the channel of the Dyfrdwy. The improvement of land by lime has of late occasioned a great consumption of coal by the farmer and by the persons who burn lime for sale.

The estuary of the Afon Dyfrdwy lies at a small distance. The tides recede here so very far as to deny us any variety of fish. The species most plentiful are the flat kind such as flounders, a few plaice, small soles, and rays. Dabs visit us in November and in the last year was taken that rare species of flounder, the whiff. The weever is very common here; other species are taken accidentally. The herring in this sea is extremely desultory. At times they appear in vast shoals, even as high as Chester, and are followed by multitudes of small vessels which enliven the channel.

Vestiges of Basingwerk Castle, in the parish of Treffynnon, appear in the foundation of a wall on the edge of Offa's ditch and on the roadside near the turnpike gate. Lord Lyttelton says that the founder was an Earl of Chester. I imagine it must have been Richard, son of Hugh Lupus and second Earl of Chester. He attempted in 1119 a pilgrimage to the well of St Wenefrede but, either in going or returning, was attacked by the Welsh and obliged to take shelter in Basingwerk. Bradshaw styles the place of his retreat an abbey, a proof that here had been a religious community before the time usually assigned for the foundation of this house. I must also draw from Lord Lyttelton's authority (for I can find no other) that this castle was demolished by the Welsh in the reign of Stephen.

Henry II in 1157, after his escape from the ambuscade of Euloe, left Basingwerk well fortified in order to secure a retreat on any future disaster. He never again trusted himself among our woods but made his marches along the open shores. This castle was but of very short duration for the gallant prince Owain Gwynedd laid siege to it in 1165, took it and levelled it to the ground, after which the name occurs no more as a fortress.

Both Llywelyn ap Iorwerth and his son Dafydd in their respective charters recite that they give and confirm the several donations to God, St Mary, the monastery of Basingwerk and the monks, which had been bestowed on them by their predecessors for the salvation of their souls. Thomas ap Dafydd Pennant presided over the abbey in the time of Gutyn Owain, a bard who flourished in the year 1480. The poet is so liberal of his praise as to say that he gave twice the treasure of a king in wine:

*Er bwrw yno, aur Brenin*
*Ef a roes, deufwy a'r win.*

Among his other luxuries, I think he enumerates sugar which a rich abbot of the 15th century might easily indulge himself in for it had been a great article of commerce in Sicily as early as the year 1148. He quitted his possession and became what is termed in law a monk deraigne, marrying about 300 years ago Angharad, daughter to Gwilym ap Gruffudd ap Gwilym of the house of Penrhyn in Gwynedd. He had by her 3 sons, the youngest of whom, Nicholas, succeeded him in the abbacy and was the last to fill the place.

The road from hence is remarkably picturesque, along a little valley bounded on one side by hanging woods beneath which the stream hurries towards the sea unless where interrupted by the frequent manufactories. Its origin is discovered at the foot of a steep hill beneath the town of Treffynnon to which it gave the name. The spring boils with vast impetuosity out of a rock and is formed into a beautiful polygonal well, covered with a rich arch supported by pillars. The roof is most exquisitely carved in stone. The resort of pilgrims of late years to these fontanalia has considerably decreased; the greatest number are from Lancashire. During the summer, a few are still to be seen in the water in deep devotion up to their chins for hours, sending up their prayers or performing a number of evolutions round the polygonal well or threading the arch between well and well a prescribed number of times.

The stream formed by this fountain runs with a rapid course to the sea which it reaches in little more than a mile's distance. The industry of this century hath made these waters of much commercial utility. The principal works at this time are battering-mills for copper; a wire-mill, coarse paper-mill, snuff-mill and a foundry for brass. A cotton manufactory is establishing, the success of which will be an extensive blessing to the neighbourhood. The town was very inconsiderable till the beginning of this century, the houses few and those for the most part thatched, they streets unpaved and the place destitute of a market. The flourishing mines that for some time were discovered in the neighbourhood made a great change in the appearance and introduced the effects of wealth. The town, or rather township, contains somewhat more than 2,000 souls.

My next visit was to Y Fflint. I took the lower road by the shore, blackened with the smoke of smelting-houses and, in the more flourishing times of the collieries, with vast stacks of coal. The last township on this side of Treffynnon parish is that of Colehill which was so called from its abundance of fossil fuel.

Y Fflint appears to have been founded in times of danger and every provision made against an attack from a people recently subdued and who had submitted reluctantly to a foreign yoke. The town is formed on the principle of a Roman encampment, being rectangular and surrounded by a vast ditch and 2 great ramparts, with 4 regular portae as usual with that military nation.

The castle stands on a low free-stone rock that juts into the sands a little north east of the town. The channel of the Dyfrdwy at present is some distance from the walls but formerly flowed beneath. There are still in some parts rings to which ships were moored. In 1280, the Welsh surprised the place at the same time that Dafydd (brother of Llywelyn) took Penarlâg, and Rhys (the son of Maelgwn) and Gruffudd ap Maredudd ap Owain seized the castle of Aberystwyth. Here in 1311, the infatuated son of our conqueror received from exile his imperious favourite Piers Gaveston who had landed at Caernarfon from Ireland.

In this dolorous castell, as Halle styles it, was deposed the unfortunate monarch Richard II. To this place he was inveigled by Henry Percy, Earl of Northumberland, with the assurance that Bolingbroke wished no more than to be restored to his own property and to give the kingdom a parliament. If Froissart may be credited, Richard did not experience the pang of ingratitude from man alone for his very dog deserted him and fawned on his rival Bolingbroke as if it understood and predicted the misfortunes of its old master.

On leaving Y Fflint, I took the road to Helygain. The prospect improves the whole way and from the heights expands to the north-east and south into an almost boundless one. The first place of any note which occurs in the parish of Helygain is a hamlet of a number of houses called the Pentre, or hamlet, a name in Wales common to all such assemblages of dwellings where there is no church (to distinguish it from

Llan where the place of devotion stands). Helygain took its rise in the present century and was much increased by the concourse of miners on the discovery of a rich vein in the adjacent fields. I cannot find that the owner of the ground, in case the mine was discovered in private property, was permitted to have any share of the profit, till the fifth of Henry VI (1426). If any gold or silver was found in the mines of baser metal, the whole would belong to the king.

Trivial accidents, even to this age, have been the cause of mighty mineral discoveries. The great mine at Helygain was discovered by ditching; that at Llangynog in Trefaldwyn by the slip of a woman ascending a hill and baring the vein with her feet. It will perhaps amuse the reader that in this county, within my memory, recourse was had to the divining rod. A foreign adventurer, half knave, half enthusiast, made the trial but it proved as unsuccessful to himself as to his admirers. Let me now return to realities!

Moel y Gaer, or the hill of the fortress, lies on the summit of a hill and is surrounded by a great fosse and dike of a circular form, with an entrance as usual to such places and a small artificial mount within the precinct from whence our ancient heroes might animate their followers. This seems to have been an outpost of the Ordovices in order to defend their country against the Roman invaders. Here our ancestry lodged their wives and children; to these places they drove their cattle out of the low country and established garrisons ready to sally forth and repel the foe. In late times this spot proved fatal to a valiant partisan of Owain Glyndŵr. Hywel Gwynedd was surprised in a negligent hour within this post and was beheaded.

Northop, a little town, bears the addition of North to distinguish it from the other Hope (Estyn). The Welsh name is Llan Eurgain, from St Eurgen (daughter of Maelgwn Gwynedd ap Caswallon Lawhir ap Einion Arth ap Cunedda Wledig who died in 586). Northop is a sinecure annexed to the bishopric of St Asaph in the 6th year of Queen Anne's reign, in order to compensate for the mortuaries due to the bishop on the death of every beneficed clergyman in the diocese. From an account taken in the reign of Queen Elizabeth, the following were customary:

His best gelding, horse or mare; his best gown; his best cloak; his best coat, jerkin, doublet and breeches; his hose or nether stockings and garters; his waist coat; his hat and cap; his sword; his best book; his surplice; his purse and girdle; his knife and gloves; his signet or ring of gold.

About a quarter of a mile out of the Chester road are the ruins of Euloe castle, placed on the edge of a deep wooded dingle. In the woods

*Hawarden Castle*

near this place, called to this day Coed Euloe, part of the flower of the army detached by Henry II in 1157 from his camp at Saltney was surprised and defeated by Dafydd and Cynan, sons of Owain Gwynedd, sent by their father with a strong party from his camp near Basingwerk. Henry later attempted to cut off Owain Gwynedd by marching along the shore and getting between him and the mountains but the wise prince, penetrating into his views, retired to a plain near Llanelwy (still called Cil-Owain or *Owain's Retreat*) and from thence to a strong post named Bryn y Pin, defended by great ramparts and ditches. This camp lies in the parish of St George on a lofty rock above the church and is now called Pen y Parc.

Within the lordship of Euloe are very considerable potteries of coarse earthen ware such as pans, jugs, great pots for butter, plates, dishes, ovens and flowerpots. There are 14 works which make annually between 3,000 and 4,000 pounds worth. The ware is mostly exported to Ireland and the towns on the Welsh coast, particularly to Abertawe. There are besides 6 other works for the making of fire bricks, few clays being better fitted for the purpose of resisting the intense heat of the smelting furnaces. Great quantities of tiles for barn floors, and for rooms, are also made here and the annual sale of these 2 articles amounts to about 1,200 pounds.

I must not leave the parish of Northop without visiting the maritime parts which stretch along the channel of the Dyfrdwy. We find there the names of certain townships taken notice of in Domesday book; Lead-brook (Normanised into Latbroc from the Anglo-Saxon Laed and Broca either from the quantity of lead washed out of it or from the smelting-works established on it.

Of late years, a very handsome pier has been built at Gwepra by the River Dee Company, jutting into the channel, for the protection of the ships bound to or from Chester, under which they may take shelter in bad weather or adverse winds.

From hence I ascended to Penarlâg, a small town. This place, like most others in our county, bears 2 names: Pennard halawg (perhaps corrupted from Pen y Llwch, or the headland above the lake) and Haordine as we find it written in Domesday book. The whole was valued at 40 shillings yet supporting but 4 villeins, 6 boors and 4 slaves, so low was the state of population. In 1264, Llywelyn, Prince of Wales, had a conference at this place with Simon de Montfort (the potent Earl of Leicester) where they established peace between Cheshire and Wales in order to promote their respective designs. In the year following, on June 22nd, Montfort obliged his captive monarch to make an absolute cession to the Welsh prince not only of this fortress but of the absolute sovereignty of Wales. After the suppression of Leicester's rebellion, Penarlâg relapsed to the crown. The castle was probably destroyed by Llywelyn himself, who foresaw the impossibility of his keeping a fortress so near the English borders. It must soon have been rebuilt for I find in 1280 it was styled Castrum Regis.

During the civil wars, this castle suffered the usual vicissitudes of fortune. It was early possessed by the parliament, being betrayed by the governor (a neighbouring gentleman of the name of Ravenscroft) and kept for parliament's use till the year 1643.

The remains are a fine circular tower or keep, on the summit of a mount. This alone is pretty entire. Nothing exists at present except this, a few walls and the foundations of some rooms which Sir John Glynne has with great pains laid open by the removal of the rubbish. In one place was discovered a long flight of steps, at the bottom of which was a door, and formerly a draw-bridge which crossed a deep long chasm (nicely faced with free-stone) to another door leading to 2 or 3 small rooms. Probably they were places of confinement where prisoners might be lodged with the utmost security.

The parish receives 200 pounds a year from the River Dee Company. This was granted by act of parliament in consideration of 800 acres of land belonging to Penarlâg, inclosed on the north side of the river for the use of adventurers in the navigation. This sum is to be payed to the lord of the manor and other trustees and is applicable to any uses which any 5 (with the consent of the lord) shall agree on.

In Broadlane, the mansion-house built by the late Sir John Glynne in 1752, are 2 portraits of the chief justice Glynne, the able political lawyer of the reign of Charles I and the succeeding usurpation. He was of the house of Glynllifon in Gwynedd which derives itself from Cilmyn Troed-ddu (Cilmyn with the black foot), one of the 15 tribes and nephew of Myrfryn Frych, Prince of Wales in the year 818.

Sir John Glynne was born at Glynllifon in the year 1602; his father was Sir William Glynne, his mother a Gruffudd of Caernarfon. His school was that of the college at Westminster; his academic learning was instilled into him at Hart-hall, Oxford, and his knowledge of the law at Lincoln's Inn where he became a bencher. His abilities were soon discovered by the popular party, by whose influence he was made steward at Westminster and recorder of London, and twice elected member for the former in the 2 parliaments of 1640. He was, next to Pym, the most active manager against the Earl of Strafford.

Close to the village of Bretton lies the large marsh of Saltney which reaches within about a mile of Chester. It is at present divided by a most excellent road by whose side runs a small canal cut by Sir John Glynne for the conveyance of his coal into the Afon Dyfrdwy near the city. This tract was formerly granted by Robert, Lord of Mold, to the monks of Basingwerk for pasturage; he also gave them the same privilege in Penarlâg and the liberty of cutting rushes for thatching their buildings.

*Roman Gate at Chester*

# Chapter Two

# Chester to Overton

ACCESS TO the city of Chester (Deva as it was named by the Romans) is over a very narrow and dangerous bridge of 7 irregular arches, till of late rendered more inconvenient by the ancient gateways at each end, formerly necessary enough to prevent the inroads of my countrymen who often carried fire and sword to these suburbs which were so frequently burnt as to be called by the Britons Treboeth or the burnt town.

Caer Lleon Fawr ar Dyfrdwy (the camp of the great legion on the Dyfrdwy) was the headquarters of the 20th legion. This legion came into Britain before the year 61 for it had its share in the defeat of Boadicea by Suetonius. After this victory, the Roman forces were led towards the borders of northern Wales, probably into this county. Afterwards, by reason of the relaxed state of discipline, a wing had been cut off by the Ordovices just before the arrival of Agricola but the quarters of these troops at this period are not exactly known. It is probable that Suetonius collected and began his march against the enemy from this place; and that, after his successful expedition into Mona, he determined to fix here a garrison as the fittest place to bridle the warlike people he was about to leave behind him. In consequence he fixed part of the legion here and detachments in the neighbouring posts before he ventured on the distant expedition to Scotland, into which he led part as appears from the inscriptions which prove that a vexillatio of this legion was concerned in building a portion of the Roman wall.

The form of the city evinces the origin to have been Roman, being in the figure of their camps with 4 gates, 4 principal streets, and variety of lesser streets crossing the others at right angles dividing the whole into lesser squares. The walls, the precincts of the present city, mark the limits of the ancient. No part of the old walls exist but they stood, like the modern, on the soft free-stone rock high above the circumjacent country.

The four principal streets run direct from east to west and north to south. They were excavated out of the earth and sunk many feet beneath the surface. The carriages were driven far below the level of the kitchens on a line with ranges of shops over which, on each side of the streets, passengers walk from end to end, secure from wet or heat, in galleries (or rows as they are called) purloined from the first floor of each house, open in front and balustraded. The back courts of all these houses are level with the rows but to go into any of these four streets it is necessary to descend a flight of several steps. These rows appear to me to have been the same with the ancient vestibules and to have been a form of building preserved from the time that the city was possessed by the Romans.

A round arch called the Ship-gate or Hole in the Wall, now filled up, seems originally designed for the common passage over the Dyfrdwy into the country of the Ordovices, either by means of a boat at high water or by fording at low, the river here being remarkably shallow. What reduces this to a certainty is that the rock on the Hanbridge side is cut down as if for the convenience of travellers. And immediately beyond, in the field called Edgar's, are the vestiges of a road pointing up the hill which was continued toward Bonium, the present Bangor Is-Coed.

In front of a rock in the same field, and facing this relic of the Roman road, is cut a rude figure of Minerva with her bird and altar. This probably was a sepulchral monument, for such were very usual on the sides of highways; but time or wantonness has erased all inscription.

Beyond this stood, past all memory, some ancient buildings whose site is marked by certain hollows; for the ground (probably over the vaults) gave way and fell in within the remembrance of persons now alive. Tradition calls the spot the site of the palace of Edgar.

I must not omit the most valuable memorial which the Romans left to this county: the art of cheese-making, for we are expressly told that the Celts were ignorant of it till the arrival of the Romans. The Cestrians have improved so highly in this article as to excel all countries, not excepting that of Italy, the land of their ancient masters.

The 20th legion was recalled from Britain before the writing of the Notitia, it not being mentioned in that work which was composed about the year 445. The city must not at that period be supposed to be totally deserted; it remained occupied by the legionaries' descendants who partook of the same privileges and were probably a numerous body. Numbers likewise who had married with the native islanders and embraced civil employs in all likelihood stayed behind after the final abdication of Britain by the legions in 448. After this the city fell under the government of the Welsh till their conquest was entirely effected by the new invaders, the Saxons.

Britain, now left defenceless, quickly experienced all the calamities that could be inflicted on it from a foreign and barbarous people. While Hengist and Horsa poured in their troops from the south, another set of banditti landed in Wales from their settlements in the Orcades and the north of Scotland. These, with their allies the Picts, were defeated near Yr Wyddgrug by the Christian Britains headed by St Germanus. The probable rest that Deva enjoyed for another century was owing to this victory which, obtained seemingly in a miraculous manner, discouraged for a long space any new attempts.

The fate of this city was at length decided in 607 when Ethelfrith, King of Northumbria, resolved to add this rich tract to his dominions. He was opposed by Brochwel Ysgythrog, King of Powys, who called to his aid one 1,200 religious from the great convent of Bangor and posted them on a hill in order that he might benefit by their prayers. Ethelfrith fell in with this pious corps and, finding out what their business was, put them to the sword without mercy. He made an easy conquest of Brochmail who, as the Saxon Chronicle informs us, escaped with about 50 men. It appears that Ethelfrith, after pillaging the city, left it to the former owners and contented himself with the territory till it was wrested from his kingdom by that of Mercia.

The Welsh seem to have continued in possession of this city and it was considered to be the capital city of Venedotia, or northern Wales, till it was finally wrested out of their hands by Egbert, about the year 828, during the reign of the Welsh prince Merfyn and his wife Esyllt, which contracted the limits of Wales during the remainder of its independent existence.

In a few years after, Chester underwent a heavy calamity from the Danes. These pirates, the scourge of the kingdom, meeting with a severe defeat by Alfred the Great, retreated before him and in their flight collected vast numbers of their countrymen. They committed the care of their wives, their ships and their booty, to the East Angles, and marched night and day to secure quarters in the west. After the evacuation of the city by the Danes, it continued in ruins till the year 907 or 908 when the Saxon Chronicle and all our ancient historians agree it was restored by the celebrated Ethelfleda, daughter of the great Alfred.

The village of Eccleston is prettily situated on the Afon Dyfrdwy and commands a view of the towers and spires of Chester rising above the wooded banks. The most extensive prospect is from a bench on Eccleston hill, on the road-side, which takes in the vast environs of Wales, Cheshire, and part of Shropshire, forming an admirable composition of rich cultivation bounded by hills of various forms. Ecclestone retains the same name which it had at the Conquest in 1066. It was held at that time by Gilbert de Venables from Hugh Lupus; before that event, by Edwin a freeman. On the demesne land were 2 servants, 4 villeyns and a boor, a boat and a net.

A little farther is Eaton, or the hamlet on the water; a name the most common of any in England. At the Conquest here was a fishery which employed 6 fishermen and yielded 1,000 salmon. This fishery has long since ceased but, during its existence, the minister of Eccleston claimed the 20th fish.

Cross the river at Eaton-boat, leaving on the right Oldford bridge, a neat structure forming another communication between the 2 parts of the hundred of Broxton which, at the time of the Conquest, bore the name of Dudestan hundred.

After riding along a dirty flat country, reach Farn or Farndon, a small town on the Dyfrdwy called in the Domesday book Ferenton. The church was burnt by the parliament army in 1645 during the siege of Holt castle and rebuilt after the cessation of the war. In one window, over the pew of the respectable family of Barnston, is some very beautiful painted glass of a commander in his tent with a truncheon in his hand, surrounded by the military instruments in use in the reign of Charles I. This town is separated from Dinbych by an ancient stone bridge of 10 arches, with the vestiges of a guard-house in the middle. The date, 1345, was preserved till very lately on a stone over the arch called the Lady's arch.

Holt, another small town, stands on an eminence on the Welsh side, an ancient borough and corporation consisting of a mayor, 2 bailiffs and a coroner. The inhabitants, with those of Ruthun and Dinbych, enjoy the privilege of sending 2 burgesses to parliament. This town is in the parish of Gresford but in the diocese of Chester. It is the only appurtenance remaining on this side of the Dyfrdwy of the vast grant made by Edward the Confessor to that see of all the land on the other side of the river, which he first gave to, and then took from, our prince Gruffudd ap Llywelyn. The poor relics of the castle are seated close to the river and are insulated by a vast fosse cut through a deep bed of soft red stone which seems originally to have been thus quarried for the building of the castle. This fortress consisted of 5 bastions, and the work cut into that form to serve as a base to as many towers. It had been defended in 3 parts by the great chasm formed by the quarry; on the fourth by the Dyfrdwy into which jutted a great quay still to be seen in the dry seasons for it has long since been covered by the encroachment of the river.

Originally this place had been a small outpost to Deva. Slopes and other now obsolete works may be seen near the castle and on the opposite side of the water. Coins have been found here that put the matter out of doubt; I have seen some of Antonius, Galienus, Constantinus and Constantius. I conjecture the Roman name was Castra Legionis and the Welsh Castell Leon or the castle of the legion because it was garrisoned by a detachment based at Chester. The English borderers might easily mistake Lleon for the plural of Llew, which signifies a lion, and so call it the castle of Lions as we find it styled when it came into possession of Earl Warren and his successors.

This country formed part of Powys. In the articles of pacification between Henry III and our last prince Llywelyn, the limits of the principality experienced but a very small diminution from what it was in Offa's time when it was agreed that the Afon Dyfrdwy should be the boundary from Wirral to Castrum Leonum (Holt) and from thence a direct line to Pengwern Powys (Shrewsbury).

The fortress of Dinas Brân was the chief residence of Gruffudd ap Madog. He unfortunately became enamoured of Emma, an English lady, daughter of James Lord Audley. Alienating his affections from his country, Gruffudd became one instrument of its subjection and of the destruction of his own family. He took part with Henry III and Edward against his natural prince. The resentment of his countrymen was raised against him and he was obliged to confine himself in his castle of Dinas Brân where probably grief and shame put an end to his life.

At a small distance from Shocklach castle, I entered Maelor Saesneg, a hundred of Fflint disjoined from the rest of the county. I took my quarters at Broughton, a venerable wooden house in possession of my respected kinsman Peter Davies in right of his lady, eldest surviving sister to the late Broughton Whitehall. The Whitehalls were originally of Staffordshire but settled here in 1663 by virtue of a marriage between Rowland Whitehall and Elizabeth daughter of John Broughton. The Broughtons derived themselves from the great Welsh stock of Tudur Trefor, Earl of Hereford, and assumed their name from this place in the reign of Henry VII.

At the back of this house lies the noted common of Threap-wood, from time immemorial a place of refuge for the frail fair who make here a transient abode clandestinely to be freed from the consequences of illicit love. Numbers of houses are scattered over the common for their reception. This tract, till of late years, had the ill-fortune to be extra-parochial, at first either because it was in the hands of irreligious or careless owners or was situated in forest or desert places; it never was united to any parish. The inhabitants therefore considered themselves as

*Holt Castle in 1610*

beyond the reach of law, resisted all government and even opposed the excise laws till they were forced to submit but not without bloodshed on the occasion. The very name speaks the manners of the dwellers. Threap-wood derived from the Anglo-Saxon Threapian, to threap, a word still in use signifying to persist in a fact or argument be it right or wrong.

On leaving Broughton, I took the road towards Bangor Is-Coed. On the right lies Emral Hall, the seat of the Pulestons; a family settled here in the time of Edward I but took their name from Pulesdon, a township in Shropshire. The first who possessed the place was Roger, a favourite officer of the king who, after the conquest of Wales, appointed him collector of the taxes raised towards the support of the war against France; but the Welsh, unused to these levies, seized on de Puleson and hanged him. His son, another Richard, held in the 7th of Edward II lands in the parish of Worthenbury, by certain services and per ammabrogium (a pecuniary acknowledgement paid by tenants to the king, or vassals to their lord, for the liberty of marrying, or not marrying). Thus Gilbert de Maisnil gave 10 marks of silver to Henry III for leave to take a wife; and Cecily, widow of Hugh Peverel, that she might marry whom she pleased. It is strange that this servile custom should be retained so long. It is pretended that the Amobyr among the Welsh, the Lyre-wite among the Saxons, and the Marcheta mulierum among the Scots, were fines paid by the vassal to the superior, to buy off his right to the first-night's lodging with the bride of the person who held from him; but I believe there never was any European nation (in the periods in which this custom was pretended to exist) so barbarous as to admit it. It is true that the power above cited was introduced into England by the Normans out of their own country. The Amobyr, or rather Gobr merch, was a British custom of great antiquity, paid either for violating the chastity of a virgin or for the marriage of a vassal and signifies the price of a virgin. The Welsh laws, so far from encouraging adultery, checked by severe fines even unbecoming liberties.

There is one species so singular as to merit mention: If a wife proved unfaithful to her husband's bed, the poor cuckold was obliged to pay his superior 5 shillings as long as he did cydgyfgu, i.e. sleep with her. But if he forbore cohabiting with her, and the cydgyfgu'd with her gallant, the fine fell on the offending fair.

Continue my journey to Bangor Is-Coed, seated on the banks of the Dyfrdwy which is here bounded on both sides by rich meadows. The church has been built at different times but no part is very ancient. This place is celebrated for being the site of the most ancient British monastery, or rather seminary, which contained 2,400 monks who,

*Coffin lids found at Bangor Is-Coed*

dividing themselves into 7 bands, passed their time alternately in prayer and labour; or, as another writer says, 100 (by turns) passed one hour in devotion so that the whole 24 hours were employed in sacred duties. This pious community was dispersed after the slaughter of their brethren at the battle of Chester, and their house overthrown.

William the monk, and librarian of Malmsbury, contemporary with King Stephen, speaks of the remains in his days, saying that no place could show greater remains of half-demolished churches and multitudes of other ruins that were to be seen in his time. The monks of this community, in common with all the British clergy, were strenuous opposers of the usurpation of the church of Rome. Seven bishops and a great number of learned men were deputed from Bangor to meet the famous missionary Augustine the monk. He insisted on their concurrence with his demands with such insolence that they left him, determined to maintain the original rites of their own church which remained pure and independent of all foreign prelates for many centuries after that period. Augustine threatened the Welsh with the resentment of the Saxons. How far he instigated Ethelfrith in this invasion does not appear but, if Bede may be depended on, the massacre of the monks almost immediately followed his menaces.

I could discover no remains of this once noted place but was informed that squared stones have been often ploughed up in a field called Stanyards, probably the site of some ancient buildings. This place has been also the site of the supposed Bonium or Bovium, a Roman station. Leland says that, in his time, Roman money was found there.

The ancient Celtic boats, the vitilia navigia of Pliny (the modern coracles), are much in use in these parts for the purposes of salmon fishing. They have now lost the cause of their name, being no longer covered with coria or hides but with strong canvas. They hold only a single person, who uses a paddle with great dexterity. The Celts had them of large size and even made short voyages in them according to the accounts we receive from Lucan.

The bridge is a beautiful light structure and consists of 5 arches. On crossing the Dyfrdwy, entered into Dinbych again and, turning short to the left, after 2 miles riding, visited Eyton, the seat of Kenrick Eyton. This house was head of a numerous race of gentry that took their name from the place so called from its situation. The Dyfrdwy rolls beneath and forms a long and solemn reach, overshadowed by hanging woods. At Overton bridge, which lies about a mile beyond Eyton, the channel is contracted and the stream flows picturesquely between lofty banks, admirably described by the inimitable pencil of Mr Sandby.

Overton, or Overton Madog, the Ovreton of the Domesday book, is a pleasant village seated on a high band about a mile beyond the bridge, above a rich meadowy flat of a semicircular form, varied by the Afon Dyfrdwy and bounded in front with fertile and wooded slopes; lofty and naked mountains soar beyond and close the scene.

An extent was made in the 28th of Edward I at Overton before Richard de Mascy, justice of Chester, by which it appears that the king had a mill there worth 12 pounds a year, and a fishery worth 20 pounds; which shows the greatness of the value of the latter in those days. The only fish worth attending to must have been salmon. It was an important article, not only in private families but, in those days, for the support of armies. In Rymer is an order for 3,000 dried salmon, issued by Edward II in 1308 to enable him to set his troops in motion to wage war against Scotland.

Gwernhailed, the seat of Mr Fletcher, in this parish, must not pass unnoticed. Few places command so rich a view and few have been more judiciously improved. Beneath runs the Dyfrdwy, bounded on the opposite side by most beautiful meadows and varied in the distance with numbers of hills, among which those of Caergwrle form a most noble and conspicuous mass.

In this neighbourhood I visited the fine collection of birds at Bryn y Pys, the seat of Richard Parry. Among others was a pair of Angolan vultures. They are now dead but one of their exuviae, stuffed so as to mimic life, is placed in the matchless Museum of Sir Ashton Leyer which is far the most instructive and elegant of any in Europe and from which the mere admirer will receive equal pleasure with the profoundest connoisseur.

I must not leave this neighbourhood without observing that the little owl (*British Zoology* volume 1 number 70), that rare English species, has been shot in some adjacent woods. It is very frequent abroad, where they collect in autumn and the spring in great flocks, in order to migrate in search of field-mice.

## Chapter Three

# From Overton, through Ellesmere to Whittington and Oswestry

**WITHIN A** small distance from Overton, I entered the country of Salop (or Shropshire) at Trench Lane, once infamous for its depth and badness. This county was peopled by the Cornavii and, till the time of Offa, divided between the princes of Powys and the Mercian kingdom; but Offa, after his expulsion of the Welsh from their ancient seat of Pengwern (or Shrewsbury), added their part to his dominions. At the Conquest, it was possessed by the brave Edwin, the last Earl of Mercia. On his death, it was bestowed by the Conqueror on Roger de Montgomery, a potent Norman, the first Earl of Arundel and Shrewsbury.

The country, for the greatest part of the way to Ellesmere, is flat, dirty and unpleasing. On the approach to the town, it becomes more agreeable and breaks into most beautiful risings, fertile and finely wooded. The bottoms are indeed destitute of rivers but frequently filled with lakes called here meres, elegantly bordered by the cultivated hills. It is singular that none of them are the parents of streams; their increase from rains and springs, and their loss by exhalations, keep such equal pace!

The town is of Saxon origin and takes its name from the water, which was called Aelfmere (or the greatest mere, being the chief in this part of the county). The place has little to boast of except its situation. The principal trade is that of malt, the barley of the neighbourhood being remarkably good.

Shrewsbury castle stood on a vast artificial mount on a rising ground with 3 great ditches on the more accessible side. At present not a vestige is to be seen, the top being formed into a bowling-green that may vie with any in England for the elegance and extent of the inland prospect, of the lake beneath, of the rich country and woods surrounding the town. At a distance: Chester and the Broxton hills, Wrecsam and the Caergwrle mountains, Castle Dinas Brân, and the Berwyn alps, and some of those of Meirionnydd; Llanymynech hill, the Breyddin, Pimhill, Cleehill and the noted Wrekin.

I cannot trace the founder of the castle nor yet the time of its destruction. The place was possessed, as I before said, by Edwin immediately before the Conquest, and on that event by Roger de Montgomery.

In 1177, it was transferred to a prince of northern Wales. Henry II in that year assembled a council at Oxford and, among other regulations for the security of the kingdom, bestowed on Dafydd ap Owain his natural sister Emma, with the lordship of Ellesmere as a portion. This the politic monarch did in hopes of retaining the affections of Dafydd and to prevent a breach with the Welsh, who gave him such great disturbance and so often baffled his greatest endeavours to subdue them during the reign of Owain Gwynedd (father to Dafydd). This alliance answered his purpose for the English remained unmolested during the life of the prince.

King John, by grant dated from Dover April 16th 1204, bestowed the castle, with Joan (his natural daughter by Agatha, daughter of Robert Ferrers Earl of Derby) on Llywelyn ap Iorwerth. It is probable that John hoped, by means of his son-in-law, to terrify the lord marchers into obedience but the unfortunate monarch reaped no benefit from the alliance. Joan proved unfaithful to our prince's bed. Llywelyn hanged William de Breos, author of his disgrace, and turned his arms against the English. This induced John to divest Llywelyn of the government of so important a fortress as a frontier castle, still leaving the revenues of the lands to his daughter. Llywelyn in revenge afterwards burnt the town.

A remarkable circumstance at this place put a stop to much cruelty exercised by ordinance of parliament against the native Irish who served in England in the royal army during the civil wars. Prince Rupert, in one of his marches across the country, halted at Ellesmere and determined, by retaliation, to revenge the deaths of the Irish sufferers; 13 of that kingdom had lately been executed by the parliament army in cool blood. Here the prince ordered the prisoners whom he had in possession to cast lots for their lives on the drum-head, and the 13 on whom the fatal destiny fell to be hanged. The die was cast and the unfortunate men selected. While preparation was making for their execution, one of them (Philip Littleton, who had been park-keeper to Robert Corbet of Stanwardine) saw Sir Vincent Corbet of Moreton Corbet ride by in the prince's army. Littleton told a soldier that he was sure Sir Vincent would intercede for him. The soldier, with great humanity, ran to the knight and informed him of the case, who immediately obtained Littleton's pardon. The rest were executed; and after this no more Irish were put to death in this kingdom.

From Ellesmere I continued my journey towards Oswestry. From an eminence called the Perthy, have a most extensive view of the flat part of the county, bounded by the hills of Dinbych, Trefaldwyn and Shropshire. Amidst them appear the vast gaps through which the Severn and the Dyfrdwy rush upon the plains out of their mountainous confinement. This tract is intermixed with woods, fertile land, and moors of great extent.

After a ride of 2 or 3 miles along the flat, reach Halston, the seat of the Myttons, my maternal ancestry; a good house built about the year 1690 with the advantage of wood and water which were managed with excellent taste by my worthy cousin the late John Mytton. The house is situated on an elevated plot of land which rises out of an extensive flat, great part of which was subject to frequent floods, an inconvenience which has since been removed by the present owner at the expense of much trouble and money in draining considerable tracts of low ground, whereby the neighbourhood is rendered more healthy and pleasant. The rest of the grounds are watered by the river Perry, a stream which used to abound with excellent pike, perch, dace, gudgeons, crayfish and eels, till modern luxury gave an additional spur to the dexterity of poachers, a grievance complained of though encouraged in this as well as in most rivers in the kingdom.

At this place was born in 1608 the famous general Thomas Mytton, a most able, active and successful commander on the part of the parliament during the civil wars. The scene of his actions was chiefly in northern Wales. By his military prowess, most of the castles in northern Wales were subdued and he greatly distinguished himself in several battles. Finding that Cromwell and his party had farther designs than the mere defence of liberty (the cause in which he engaged), he resigned his command and retired.

Mr William Mytton's curious manuscripts of the Shropshire antiquities are preserved here; to his labours I owe frequent obligations in this part of the work.

The name Halston imports something of sanctity, signifying the Holy Stone. A cross or stone, the object of superstition, might once have stood here but that and its legend are quite lost. That it had been a sanctuary is evident. In the reign of Richard I, Meurig Llwyd (descended from Hedd Molwynog, one of the 15 tribes of northern Wales), became indignant at certain injuries done his country by the introduction of new laws and new customs. He seized several of the king's officers, slew some and hung others. He fled the rage of his enemies and took refuge at this place.

At a mile's distance, I reached Whittington, a village of 94 families seated in a parish of the same name. The number of families in the whole amounts to 275. The population has of late increased pretty much. The addition to the numbers in the parish has chiefly been confined to the village, owing to the several houses built for the convenience of labourers by the family of the Myttons; which evinces the duty and utility of rural residence in our gentry, by promoting population and cherishing the industrious poor.

Mr Lloyd, in his Archeologia, imagines this place might have been celebrated under the name of Dref Wen, (*the White Town*), by Llywarch Hen, a noble bard of the race of the Cumbrian Britons, who flourished in the year 590. Here, says he, was slain Condolanus, a chieftain of his country, in an attempt to expel a set of invaders:

*Y Dref Wen ym mron y coed:*
*Yfeu yu y hevras erioed:*
*Ar wyneb y gwelht y gwaed.*
*Y Dref Wen yn yd hymyr*
*Y hevras y glâs vyvyr*
*Y gwaed y dan draed y gwŷr.*

Some part of this is too obsolete to be translated. It expresses in general the rage of battle and that the grass under the feet of the warriors was stained with blood. Our bards also make this place the property and chief seat of Tudur Trefor, a Welsh nobleman who lived in the year 924 and in right of his mother Rheingar, granddaughter and heiress of Caradog-Freichfras. Caradog was slain by the Saxons in the battle of Rhuddlan in 795.

After leaving the village, in the road towards Oswestry, I observed on the left Trenewydd, a seat of Watkin Williams in the right of his mother, heiress of the place. Her grandfather, Edward Lloyd, who died in 1715, was eminent for his learning and had prepared materials for the history of this, his native country.

Continue my journey to Oswestry (a considerable town about 2 miles from Whittington) celebrated in Saxon history and legendary piety. On this spot, on August 5th 642, was fought the battle between the Christian Oswald, King of the Northumbrians, and the pagan Penda,

King of the Mercians. Oswald was defeated and lost his life. The barbarian victor cut the body of the slain prince into pieces and stuck them on stakes dispersed over the field, as so many trophies.

It is probable that the Welsh bestowed on the spot where the battle was fought the name of Maes Hir, or the long field (or long combat, from the obstinacy of the conflict). The Saxons for a considerable time retained the name of the place where the action was fought, with the addition of their own vernacular word feld (or felth), a field, as maserfeld, maserfelth and corruptly masafeld. In after-days, the name became entirely Saxon and from the fate of the king was styled Oswald's tree, now Oswestry, and by the Welsh Croes-oswallt. Before this event, and for a long space beyond, this tract was the property of the Welsh till it was conquered by Offa and brought within the verge of his famous ditch.

A prince so dear to the church as Oswald, and so attached to the professors of the monastic life, received every posthumous honour that they could bestow. He was raised to the rank of a saint and his sanctity confirmed by numberless miracles. His relics (which were removed the year following by Oswy) were efficacious in all disorders incident to man or beast. A church arose on the place of the martyrdom, dedicated to the saint. A monastery was founded which bore the name of Blanc-minster, Candida ecclesia, Album monasterium, and White-minster. It is very singular that no evidences exist, either of the time of the foundation or the dissolution. Some writers entertain doubts whether this place was the Album Monasterium visited by Giraldus and endeavour to fix it at Whitchurch. The present church is of no great antiquity, is spacious and has a handsome plain tower. Part of this parish still uses the Welsh language.

The town was fortified with a wall and 4 gates. That called Black-gate is demolished; the New-gate, the Willow-gate and the Beatrice gate still remain. The walls were begun in the year 1277, or the 6th of Edward I who granted a murage of toll on the inhabitants of the county which lasted for 6 years in which time it may be supposed they were completed. There are only a few fragments of the castle remaining. Our Welsh historians attribute the foundation to Madog ap Maredudd ap Bleddyn, Prince of Powys, in 1148. Leland gives some colour to this by saying that in his time there was a tower called Madog's but the English records place it in the possession of Alan, a noble Norman who received it immediately from William the Conqueror on his accession. This Alan was the stock of the Fitz-alans, earls of Arundel, which flourished (with fewer checks than usual with greatness) for near 500 years.

I will not tire the reader with a dry list of the successors to this place,

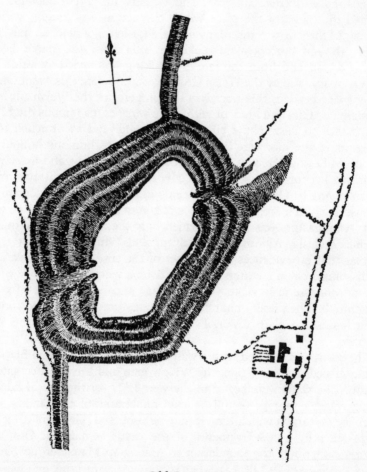

*Old Oswestry*

or the guardians of such who were under age. I will only observe that, after the execution of Edmund Earl of Arundel in the reign of Edward II, his queen, to show her predilection to her gentle Mortimer, obtained the possession of it for that favourite.

The town was favoured with considerable privileges from its lords. Its first charter, from its brevity called by the Welsh Shartar Gwtta, or the short charter, was granted by William Earl of Arundel in the reign of Henry II. It imparted to the burgesses the same privileges as those of Shrewsbury. William's son John took part with the barons against King John who in revenge marched to Oswestry in 1216 and reduced the town to ashes. On the death of that prince, he was reconciled to his successor Henry III and in 1227 obtained for his manor of Blanminster the grant of a fair upon the eve, the day, and the day after the feast of St Andrew. He also made the bailiffs clerks of the market, with power to imprison any persons who used fraudulent ways in buying or selling, for which they payed the consideration of 20 marks. These people frequently abused their power; it is therefore no wonder that so many of the grievances which the Welsh so much complained of to Edward I should originate from this place.

In 1233, this unfortunate town experienced a second destruction, being again burnt by Llywelyn ap Iorwerth, Prince of Wales. Provision was now made against future insults for, in the next reign (that of Edward I), the town was surrounded with walls.

About a mile from Oswestry, in the parish of Sellatyn, lies a fine military post on an insulated eminence of an oblong form which has been fortified with much art. The top is an extensive area containing 15 acres, 3 roods and 8 perches of fertile ground, surrounded with 2 ramparts and fosses of great heights and depths. This place is called Old Oswestry, Hen Dinas, and anciently Caer Ogyrfan (from Ogyrfan, a hero co-existent with Arthur. The strength and labour in forming it evince that it was not a sudden operation like that of a camp. Its construction, even to the oblong trenches, is Celtic. Bryn y Clawddian on the Clwydian hills, which divide Fflint from the vale of Clwyd, is a similar work.

A great dike and fosse called Wat's is continued from each side of this post. This work is little known notwithstanding it is equal in depth, though not in extent, to that of Offa. This work is little known, notwithstanding it is equal in depth, though not in extent, to that of Offa. We shall here trace the course of each. Wat's can only be discovered on the southern part to Maesbury mill in Oswestry parish, where it is lost in morassy ground. From thence it takes a northern direction to Hen-ddinas and by Pentre'r Clawdd to Gobowen, the site of a small fort called Bryn y Castell, in the parish of Whittington. It then crosses Prys Henlle common in the parish of St Martin, goes over the Ceiriog between Bryncynallt and Pont y Blew forge, and the Dyfrdwy below Nant y Bela. From thence it passes through Wynnstay park, by another Pentre'r Clawdd (township on the ditch) to Erddig, the seat of Philip Yorke, where there was another strong fort on its course. From Erddig it goes above Wrecsam, near Felin Puleston, to Rhydin in Fflint. It is often confounded with Offa's ditch which attends the former at unequal distances, from 500 yards to 3 miles, till the latter is totally lost.

Offa's ditch extended from the Wye, along the counties of Hereford and Maesyfed, into that of Trefaldwyn where I shall take it up at its entrance into North Wales at Pwll y Piod, an ale-house on the road between Bishop's Castle and Y Trenewydd. From thence it passes northward, near Mellington-hall (near which is an encampment called Caer Din), by Brompton mill where there is a mount, Linor park near Trefaldwyn, Forden heath, Nant-cribba at the foot of an ancient fortress, Layton-hall and Buttington church. Here it is lost for 5 miles, the channel of the Severn probably serving for that space as a continuation of this famous boundary which appears again just below the conflux of the Bele and the Severn, and passes by the churches of Llandysilio and Llanymynech to the edge of the vast precipitous limestone rock in the last parish. From this place it runs by Tref y Clawdd, over the horse-course on Cefn y Bwlch, above Oswestry, then above Selattyn, from whence it descends to the Ceiriog, and thence to Glyn where there is a large breach, supposed to be the place of interment of the English who fell in the battle of Crogen. It then goes by Y Waun castle and, below Cefn y Wern, crosses the Dyfrdwy and the Ruabon road near Plas Madog. It forms part of the turnpike-road to Wrecsam, to Pentre Bychan where there is a mount, then by Plas Bower to Adwy'r Clawdd near Mwynglawdd. By Brymbo it crosses Afon Cegidog river and goes through a little valley on the south side of Bryn Yorkyn mountain to Coed Talwrn and Caedwn, a farm near Treuddin chapel in the parish of Yr Wyddgrug (pointing towards the Clwydian hills) beyond which no further traces can be discovered.

The termination is remote from any hill or place of strength; it is therefore reasonable to imagine that this mighty attempt was suddenly interrupted by some cause of which we must ever remain ignorant.

The weakness of this great work appeared on the death of Offa. The Welsh, with irresistible fury, despised his toils and carried their ravages far and wide on the English marches. Superior force often repelled our countrymen. Sanguinary laws were made by the victorious Harold against any that should transgress the limits prescribed by Offa. The Welshman that was found in arms on the Saxon side of the ditch was to lose his right hand.

It is observable that, in all parts, the ditch is on the Welsh side and that there are numbers of small artificial mounts (the sites of small forts) in many places along its course. These were garrisoned and seem intended for the same purposes as the towers in the famous Chinese wall, to watch the motions of the neighbours and to repel the hostile incursions.

It is remarkable that Wat's dike should have been overlooked, or confounded with that of Offa, by all writers except the poet Thomas Churchyard who assigns the object of the work: that the space between the 2 was free ground where the Britons and Saxons might meet with safety for all commercial purposes.

From Oswestry I took the road to Sellatyn, a parish consisting of the single township of Porkington and containing about 600 inhabitants. Its register commences in 1557 and was fortunately saved from the great wreck of such records in the civil wars by Mr Wilding, an Oliverian rector. A happy disproportion of increase between births and burials seems to arise from the hilly situation of the parish. The improvements in agriculture contribute much to retain numbers of the inhabitants by finding them a wholesome and innocent employ, the want of which exiles multitudes in many places to the vice and disease of great cities.

In Sellatyn parish is Porkington, the seat of my kinsman Robert Godolphin Owen. This place takes its name from a singular entrenchment in a neighbouring field, called Castell Brogyntyn, a fort belonging to Owain Brogyntyn, a natural son to Madog ap Maredudd Prince of Powys Fadog. It is of a circular form, surrounded with a vast earthen dike and a deep foss. It appears, by an old drawing in Mr Mytton's collection, to have had 2 entrances, pretty close to each other, projecting a little from the sides, and diverging; the end of each guarded by a semi-lunar curtain. These are now destroyed.

The name of the house was soon altered to one very nearly resembling the present. In 1218, Henry III, in an address to Llywelyn Prince of Wales, informs him that among others Bleddyn Filius Oeni de Porkinton had performed to his majesty the service he owed.

Sir John Owen, the famous royalist, was of this house but not of the family of Owain Brogyntyn. He was descended from Hwfa ap Cynddelw, one of the 15 tribes of North Wales. Before Sir John Owen's family enjoyed the place, it had been long possessed by the Lacons. It passed from them to Sir William Morris of Clenennau in Gwynedd, by virtue of his marriage with the daughter of William Wynne Lacon, and was conveyed into the family of the present owner by the marriage of the grand-daughter of that match with John, 4th son of Robert Owen of Bô in Ynys Môn. This gentleman (who was father of Sir John) had been secretary to the great Walsingham and made a fortune of 10,000 pounds, a sum perhaps despised by modern secretaries but a vast one in those days. His master did not take such good care of himself for he did not leave sufficient to defray his funeral expenses.

A strenuous supporter of Charles I, Sir John was colonel in the army, and vice-admiral of North Wales. He greatly signalised himself at the siege of Bristol when it was taken by prince Rupert, and was desperately wounded in the attack. Congenial qualities recommended him to his highness who, in 1645, constituted Sir John commander of Conwy castle in place of Archbishop Williams. The fortress was soon given up to General Mytton by the contrivance of the prelate and the power of his friends, and the knight retired to his seat in the distance parts of the county. In 1648 he rose in arms to make a last effort in behalf of his fallen master, probably in concert with the royalists in Kent and Essex. He was soon attacked by William Lloyd, sheriff of the county, whom he defeated, wounded and made prisoner. He then laid siege to Caernarfon but, hearing that certain of the parliament forces, under the colonels Carter and Twistleton, were on the march to attack him, he hastened to meet them and took the sheriff with him on a litter. He met with his enemies near Llandegai. A furious recontre ensued in which Sir John had at first the advantage but fortune declared against him. In a personal contest with a Captain Taylor, he was pulled off his horse and made prisoner. His troops, disheartened by the loss of their commander, took to flight. The sheriff died the same day. The victory was esteemed of such consequence that captain Taylor, who was the messenger of the news to the parliament, received a reward of 200 pounds out of Sir John's estate.

Sir John was conveyed to Windsor castle where he found 4 noblemen under confinement for the same cause. Sir John showed a spirit worthy of his country. He told his judged that "he was a plain gentleman of Wales who had been always taught to obey the king; that he had served him honestly during the war and, finding many honest men endeavoured to raise forces whereby he might get him out of prison, he did the like". In the end he was condemned to lose his head for which, with a humorous intrepidity, he made the court a low reverence and gave his humble thanks. A bystander asked what he meant; he replied aloud: "It was a great honour to a poor gentleman of Wales to lose his head to such noble lords for by God he was afraid they would have hanged him".

Sir John, by mere good fortune, was disappointed of the honour he was flattered with. He neither solicited for a pardon nor was any petition offered to parliament in his favour though it was strongly importuned in behalf of his fellow-prisoners. Ireton proved his advocate and told the house "That there was one person for whom no one spoke a word, and therefore requested that he might be saved by the sole motive and goodness of the house". In consequence, mercy was extended to him and, after a few months imprisonment, he was, on his petition, set at liberty. He retired again into his country where he died in 1666 and was interred in the church of Penmorfa in Gwynedd.

# Chapter Four

# Chirk to Llangollen, Wrecsam, Glyndyfrdwy and Llanarmon

ON APPROACHING the village of Y Waun is a very deep valley consisting of fertile meadows watered by the brook Ceiriog and finely bounded by the lofty wooded banks. Two artificial mounts here I imagine to have been Saxon and coeval with the great labour of Offa which runs at a small distance from them.

In the deep valley which winds along the foot of the vast Berwyn mountains was a bloody conflict between part of the forces of Henry II and the Welsh in 1165. Henry had determined once more to attempt the subjection of Wales and to revenge the ravages carried through the borders by its gallant prince Owain Gwynedd. For that end, Henry assembled a vast army at Oswestry. Owain, on the contrary, collected all his chieftains, with the dependants, at Corwen. Hearing that his antagonist was so near, the king resolved to bring the matter to a speedy decision. He marched towards him, directing his vanguard to make the passage clear by cutting down the trees in order to secure himself from ambuscade. The pikemen and flower of his army were posted to cover the workmen. The spirit of the common soldiers of the Welsh army grew indignant at this attempt and, without the knowledge of their officers, they fell with unspeakable fury on these troops. The contest was violent; numbers of brave men perished. In the end, the Welsh retired to Corwen. Henry gained the summit of the Berwyn but was so distressed by the dreadful rains, and by the activity and prudence of Owain who cut him off from all supplies, that he was obliged to return ingloriously with great loss of men and equipage. The place is still called Adwy'r Beddau or the Pass of the Graves of the men who were slain here.

Before the foundation of the present castle stood another, called

Castell Crogen, and the territory around bore the name of Tref y Waun, the property of the lords of Dinas Brân. It continued in their possession till the death of Gruffudd ap Madog, a strenuous partisan of Henry III and Edward I. This exalted pile has much to boast of in its vast view into 17 counties, a most elegant and varied extent.

Repassing through the castle-gate, I recollect a barbarous privilege, retained longer in this country than in other parts of Britain: that of exempting from capital punishment even the most atrocious assassin by payment of a certain fine. This was practised by the lord marchers of these parts in the 15th century and continued in Mawddwy in Meirionnydd till it was abolished in the 27th of Henry VIII.

The Welsh Gwerth was not only a compensation for murder or homicide but for all species of injuries. To cuckold the prince was expiated at a very high rate. The offender was fined a gold cup and cover as broad as high majesty's face and a thick as a ploughman's nail who had ploughed 9 years, and a rod of gold as tall as the king and as thick as his little finger, 100 cows for every cantref he ruled over, and a white bull with different coloured ears to every 100 cows.

The recompense to a virgin who had been seduced is a very singular. On complaint made that she was deserted by her lover, it was ordered by the court that she was to lay hold of the shaven and well greased tail of a 3 years old bull, introduced through a wicker-door. Two men were to goad the beast. If she could by dint of strength retain the bull, she was to have it by way of satisfaction. If not, she got nothing but the grease that remained in her hands. I fear that the crime was not held by my countrymen to be of a very deep dye.

On leaving the castle, I ascended the front of Cefn Ucha, amidst the magnificent and flourishing plantations that arise under the direction of the present owner. This lofty hill extends towards Llangollen and affords a prospect uncommonly great. The distant view is boundless. One side impends over a most beautiful valley watered by the Dyfrdwy, diversified with groves and bounded towards the end by barren and naked rocks, tier above tier.

Descend towards Llangollen, seated in the river, environed by lofty mountains. Enjoy a beautiful ride by the side of the Dyfrdwy. On the opposite bank, Trefor house makes a handsome appearance. Below it, almost at the water edge, is a grotesque ancient house, once the property of the Foulkes.

Llangollen is a small and poor town seated in a most romantic spot near a pretty common watered by the Dyfrdwy which runs with great passion through the valley. The mountains soar to a great height above

47

their wooded basis and one, whose summit is crowned with the ancient castle Brân, is uncommonly grand. I know of no place in northern Wales where the refined lover of picturesque scenes can give a fuller indulgence to his inclination. No place abounds more with various rides or solemn walks. From this central spot, he may (as I have done) visit the seats of Owain Glyndŵr, and the fine valleys of the Dyfrdwy to its source beyond the great Llyn Tegid, or pass the mountains to the fertile vale of Clwyd, or make the tour of Wrecsam, or visit the places which I have just left. The walks along the banks of the Dyfrdwy, the venerable remains of the neighbouring abbey and the arduous ascent of Castell Dinas Brân are so engaging that I believe no traveller of taste will think a repetition of them tedious.

Leland speaks of Dinas Brân as a demolished place and adds that an eagle built annually in the neighbouring rocks; that a person was wont to be lowered down in a basket to take the young and was obliged to have another basket over his head to save him from the fury of the old birds.

The church of Llangollen is dedicated to St Collen, a descendent of Cunedda Wledig, by Ethni (daughter to Matholwch, Lord of Cwl in the kingdom of Ireland). The bridge is one of the Tri Thlws Cymru (*Three Beauties of Wales*) but more remarkable for its situation than structure. It consists of 5 arches whose widest does not exceed 28 feet in diameter. The river usually runs under only one where it has formed a black chasm of vast depth into which the water pours with great fury from a high broken ledge in the smooth a solid rock which composes the whole bed of the river. The view through the arches, either upwards or downwards, is extremely picturesque.

After a short repose, I made an excursion to Ruabon, a few miles from Llangollen. The church is dedicated to St Mary and has lately been fitted up in a very neat manner chiefly at the expense of Sir Watkin Williams Wynn who bestowed on it an organ, and a small font on occasion of the christening of his eldest son in 1772. On one side of the altar is a noble monument to the late Sir Watkin, whose virtues are still fresh in the minds of his countrymen. A fall from his horse on September 26th 1749 deprived the world of a useful citizen.

The park of Wynnstay reaches to the village of Ruabon and is most advantageously situated. Nant y Bele (*the Dingle of the Martin*) lies about a mile from hence and merits a visit from every traveller The house has been built at various times. The most ancient part is a gateway of wood and plaster dated 1616. The former name of the place was Wat-stay, from its situation on the famous dike, but was changed to the present by Sir John Wynn out of respect to his own name. It was originally called simply Ruabon and had been the residence of Madog ap Gruffudd Maelor, founder of Valle Crucis. I reserve further mention of Sir John Wynn of Gwydir till I arrive at his ancient seat.

Part of the turnpike road towards Wrecsam is formed for a considerable way along the top of the dike, which shows its prodigious thickness. A fierce battle was fought near this place between Owain Cyfeiliog Prince of Powys and the English, attended with victory to the ancient Britons, which gave rise to a beautiful poem called Hirlas Owain (*The Drinking Horn of Owain*) composed by the prince himself.

I pursued the track of Wat's dike and soon reached Erddig where small but strong entrenchments compose what is called the Roman fort but there are neither coins or anything else to confirm the conjecture of its having been one. A fragment of wall cemented with mortar is all that remains of this castelet.

Erddig originally belonged to an old Welsh family of the same name, descended I think from Tudur Trefor.

Wrecsam lies at a small distance from Erddig. This town is the largest in northern Wales, and the parish the most populous. It appears by the ancient name to have been of Saxon origin, being called Wrightesham, and Wrightelesham. I can trace it no farther back than the time of the last Earl Warren who had a grant of it. Leland speaks of it as a place where there were some merchants and good buckler-makers. Near the place is a great foundry for cannon under the direction of Mr Wilkinson who supplies many parts of Europe; in the late war between the Russians and Turks, he furnished both parties with this species of logic.

The church of Wrecsam is the glory not only of the place but of northern Wales. Hugh Bellot, vicar of Gresffordd and afterwards Bishop of Bangor and of Chester, lies in his robes recumbent near the altar. It is reported that he had so strict a veneration for the celibacy of the priesthood as never to permit a woman to inhabit or lie in his house. Two casualties are recorded to have befallen this building: the steeple was blown down on St Catherine's day 1331 and the church was burnt down about the year 1457. In order to rebuild it, an indulgence of 40 days for 5 years was granted to every contributor to so pious a work. It was finished a little before the year 1472 and glazed, according to an account I received from a friend, with glass from Normandy. The steeple, as appears by a date on it, was not finished till 1506.

The free-school is endowed with 10 pounds a year, paid by the mayor of Chester, being the bequest of Valentine Broughton, alderman of the city, for the instruction of 12 boys. The western part of this parish is hilly and mineral. Part of the mines on the waste are the property of Lord

Grosvenor and some belong to the corporation of Chester. Brymbo, another township on the heights, produces coal. In this place the inhabitants of Holt had, by the charter granted to them in 1410 by Thomas Earl of Arundel, the liberty of digging for turf and coals.

From Wrecsam I made an excursion to Gresffordd and on my road called at Acton, the seat of my good friend Ellis Yonge. This place was formerly the property of the Jeffries, a race that, after running uncontaminated from an ancient stock, had the disgrace of producing in the last century George Jeffries, chancellor of England, a man of first-rate abilities in his profession but of a heart subservient to the worst of actions. He was extremely given to the bottle and paid so little respect to his character that one day, having drunk to excess with the lord treasurer and others, they were going to strip and get upon a sign-post to drink the king's health had not they been prevented. He died in the Tower on April 18th 1689, either from hard drinking or a broken heart, and so was preserved from the infamy of public execution.

Gresffordd, or Croesffordd (*the road of the cross*) lies about 2 miles further. The church is seated on the brow of a lofty eminence over a beautiful little valley whose end exhibits a view of uncommon elegance.

Returning through Wrecsam to my quarters at Llangollen, I took a ride next morning to view the country that lies to the south-west. After a descent of no great length, enter Meirionnydd, into that portion for ever to be distinguished in the Welsh annals on account of the hero it produced who made such a figure in the beginning of the 15th century. This tract was anciently a comot in the kingdom of Mathraval, or Powys, and still retains its former title Glyndyfrdwy or the valley of the Dyfrdwy. It extend about 17 miles in length, is narrow, fertile in grass, bounded by lofty hills, often clothed with trees, and lies in the parishes of Llangollen, Llandysilio, Llansantffraid and Corwen.

This tract once belonged to the lords of Dinas Brân. After the murder of the 2 eldest sons of Gruffudd ap Madog, the last lord, the Earl Warren, who had usurped the property of the eldest, appears to have been seized with remorse for his crime and, instead of removing the object of his fear, as a Machiavellian politician would have done, procured from Edward I a grant of this tract to Gruffudd Fychan, third brother to the unhappy youth, dated from Rhuddlan February 12th 1282.

Owain Glyndŵr was 4th in descent from this nobleman. His father's name was Gruffudd Fychan, his mother's Elena (of royal blood and from whom he afterwards claimed the throne of Wales). She was eldest daughter of Thomas ap Llywelyn ap Owain, by his wife Elinor Goch, or Elinor the red, daughter and heiress to Catherine, one of the daughters of

Llywelyn last Prince of Wales. She probably was concealed by some friend on the death of her father, otherwise the jealousy of Edward about the succession would have made her share the fate of her sister Gwenllian who perforce took the veil in the convent of Shaftesbury.

Writers vary in the account of the day of the birth of Glyndŵr. One manuscript fixes it on May 28th 1354; that preserved by Lewis Owen places the event 5 years earlier, for the year 1349, says he, was distinguished by the first appearance of the pestilence in Wales and by the birth of Owain Glyndŵr. Glyndŵr appears to have had a liberal education. His ambition overcame the prejudices of his country against the English and determined him to seek preferment among them. He entered himself in the inns of court and studied there till he became a barrister. It is probable that he quitted his profession for we find that he was appointed scutiger, or squire of the body, to Richard II whose fortunes he followed to the last, was taken with him in Y Fflint castle and retired to his patrimony in Wales, with full resentment of his sovereign's wrong, when the king's houschold was dissolved. I judge that he was knighted before the deposal of his master for I find him under the title of Sir Owen de Glendore among the witnesses in the celebrated cause between Sir Richard le Scrope and Sir Robert le Grosvenour, about a coat of arms. His brother also appears there by the name of Tudor de Glendore. This cause lasted 3 years and ended in 1389.

Iolo Goch, the celebrated poet of this period, resided here for some time. He came on a pressing invitation from Owain who, knowing the mighty influence of this order of men over the ancient Celts, made his house a sanctuary for bards. He made them the instrument of his future operations and to prepare the minds of the people against the time of his intended insurrection. From Iolo I borrow the description of the seat of the chieftain when it was in full splendour. He compares it, in point of magnificence, to Westminster abbey and informs us that it had a gate-house and was surrounded with a moat. Within were 9 halls, each furnished with a wardrobe (filled, i imagine, with the clothes of his retainers according to the custom of those days). On a verdant bank was a wooden house supported on posts and covered with tiles. It contained 4 apartments, each subdivided into 2, designed to lodge the guests. Here too was a church in form of a cross, with several chapels.

The seat was surrounded with every convenience for good living and every support to hospitality: a park, warren and pigeon-house; a mill, orchard and vine-yard; and fish-pond filled with pike and gwyniads, the last introduced from the lake at Bala. A heronry, which was concomitant to the seat of every great man, supplied game for the sport of falconry.

A place still remains that retains the name of Owain's park. It extends about a mile or two beyond the site of his house, on the left hand of the valley. The vestiges of the house are small. The moat is very apparent: the measurement of the area it inclosed is 46 paces by 26. There is the appearance of a wall on the outside, which was continued to the top of a great mount on which stood the wooden house. On the other side, but at a greater distance, I had passed by another mount of the same kind, called Hêndom. This perhaps was the station of a guard to prevent surprise or insult from the English side. He had much to apprehend from the neighbouring fortress of Dinas Brân and its appendages, possessed by the Earl of Arundel, a strenuous supporter of the house of Lancaster.

The bard speaks feelingly of the wine, the ale, the braget, and the white bread; nor does he forget the kitchen, nor the important officer, the cook, whose life was estimated by our laws at 126 cows. Such was the hospitality of this house that the place of porter was useless, nor were locks of bolts known. To sum up all, no one could be hungry or dry in Sycharth, the name of the place.

In the very first year of the reign of Henry of Lancaster, Henry IV, Glyndŵr experienced the frowns of the court. Reginald Lord Grey of Ruthun, taking advantage of the disposal of Richard, instantly seized on a certain common called Croeseu which Glyndŵr, in a former reign, had recovered from him by course of law. Owain sought justice without having recourse to violence: he laid his case before parliament but his suit was dismissed without redress. This insult was aggravated by another injury. When Henry went on expedition against the Scots, Owain was to have been summoned, among other barons, to attend the king with his vassals. The writ for that purpose was delivered to Reginald who designedly neglected to deliver it till the time was nearly elapsed and it became impossible for him to obey. Reginald returned to the king and misrepresented the absence of Owain as an act of wilful disobedience and, by this piece of treachery, invaded such parts of Glyndŵr's estates as lay adjacent to his own under pretence of forfeiture.

Glyndŵr first appeared in arms in the summer of the year 1400. He directed his attack against the lands of his enemy Lord Grey, during Grey's absence, and immediately recovered what he had unjustly been disposed of. As soon as the news reached Henry, he sent Lord Talbot and Lord Grey to reduce him. They arrived with such speed that they surrounded his house before he had any notice, but he had the good fortune to escape into the woods. He immediately raised a powerful band of men and, after causing himself to be proclaimed Prince of Wales, on September 20th, surprised, plundered and burnt to the ground the town of Ruthun at the time a fair was held there. After which he retired to his fastnesses among the mountains. One I imagine to have been of great strength, surrounded by a vast rampart of stones, near Corwen, called Caer Drewyn.

Henry marched in person against Owain and penetrated as far as the Ynys Môn, putting to the sword all who resisted. The king returned without effecting any material action for, on his approach, Owain retired among the Eryri hills.

Glyndŵr's fortune and interest lay both in North and South Wales. In summer 1401 he marched with 120 men or arms and posted himself on Pumlumon hill, a lofty mountain admirably adapted for receiving succours from his vassals and friends. From hence his followers made plundering excursions and were the terror of all who declined espousing his cause. The county of Trefaldwyn suffered greatly. He sacked the capital town, burnt the suburbs of Pool and ravaged all the borders. He destroyed the abbey of Cwmhir in Maesyfed, took the castle of Radnor and caused the whole garrison, to the number of 60, to be beheaded on the brink of the castle-yard. The provocation to this piece of cruelty does not appear.

Henry marched a second time in person, entering Wales about the beginning of June. He destroyed the abbey of Ystrad Fflur in Ceredigion and ravaged the country but was obliged to make a disgraceful retreat after his forces had suffered greatly by famine and the great fatigues they continually underwent.

1402 was ushered in with a comet which the bards interpreted as an omen favourable to the cause of Glyndŵr.

Lord Grey was the first who felt the effects of Owain's power. That nobleman (strongly attached to Henry and impatient of the injuries which he and his friends received from Glyndŵr) raised a considerable army but was defeated and taken fast-bound into confinement amidst the savage fastnesses of the Eryri hills. He remained for a long time in captivity nor did he gain his liberty till he paid the vast sum of 10,000 marks. No sooner was he released than he married Jane, third daughter of the furious chieftain. He had no issue by this lady. The match was probably compulsive, at best political. He even lived to serve in the French wars in the reign of Henry V and his successor, and died in the year 1440.

The castle of Caernarfon was so closely blocked up by the friends of Glyndŵr that Ieuan ap Maredudd, happening to die there at that time, had to be removed by sea for interment in the parish church of Penmorfa on the other side of the county.

Hywel Sele of Nannau in Meirionnydd, first cousin to Owain, had a harder fate. He was, like Ieuan, an adherent to the house of Lancaster. Owain and this chieftain had long been at variance. The abbot of Cymer near Dolgellau brought them together in hopes of reconciling them and to all appearance effected this charitable design. While they were walking out, Owain observed a doe feeding and told Hywel, who was reckoned the best archer of his days, that there was a fine mark for him. Hywel bent his bow and, pretending to aim at the doe, suddenly turned and discharged the arrow full at the breast of Glyndŵr who fortunately had armour beneath his clothes so received no hurt. Enraged at this treachery, he seized on Sele, burnt his house and hurried him from the place; nor could ever any one learn how he was disposed of. Forty years after, the skeleton of a large man such as Hywel was discovered in the hollow of a great oak in which Owain was supposed to have immured him in reward for his perfidy. The ruins of the old house are to be seen in Nannau park, a mere compost of cinders and ashes.

Henry was alarmed at the successes of Glyndŵr and resolved to march in person against him once more. He issued writs to the lieutenants of Nottingham and Derby, and to those of 32 other counties, requiring them to attend him at Lichfield on July 7th in order to suppress this dangerous revolt. Before the king could assemble his forces, news arrived of Glyndŵr's victory on June 22nd over Sir Edmund Mortimer. The design of assembling his army at Lichfield was laid aside. It was resolved to distract the Welsh by 3 invasions from different quarters. The rendezvous of the first army was to be at Shrewsbury, to be commanded by the king in person; the second at Hereford, to be assembled by Edmund Earl of Stafford, Richard Earl of Warwick, and the Lords Grey, Abergavenny, Audeley and Berkeley; and the third, under the conduct of prince Henry, at Chester. The forces were to be assembled at each place by the 27th of August.

Owain, assured that these preparations could not take effect till a certain time, gave loose to his resentment in the beginning of August against the inhabitants of Morgannwg who had sided with the English. After burning the bishop's castle and the archdeacon's house at Llandaf, he likewise burnt Cardiff and Abergavenny and then returned to make head against the English.

The Scots, at this time, took advantage of the commotions of the Welsh and, under the command of the great Douglas, invaded England with a body of 12,000 or 13,000 men. Henry had intelligence that it was to take place on the assumption of the blessed Virgin, or the 15th of August, and directed the lieutenant of the county of Lincoln to hasten towards the north with all the men he could raise.

Henry during this time proceeded on his expedition against the Welsh. Glyndŵr, who had too much prudence to hazard a battle against so superior an army, retired to the fastnesses of the mountains, driving away the cattle and destroying every means the English had of subsistence. A continued course of storms and rains, with the continual watching against an enemy hovering over them and ready to take every occasion of calling on them from the heights, wasted the army with sickness and fatigue. The king was obliged once more to make a most inglorious retreat. News from the north served to alleviate the ill success of Henry's invasion; a complete victory was won over the Scots on Homeldon hill near Wooler.

Glyndŵr was now in the meridian of his glory. Assembled the estates of Wales at Machynlleth, a town of Trefaldwyn, he caused there his title to the principality to be acknowledged and was formally crowned. At this meeting he narrowly escaped assassination by his brother-in-law, a gentleman of Brychciniog, Dafydd Gam, or the one-eyed. The plot was discovered. Dafydd was arrested and imprisoned in close confinement until the year 1412.

An open war was daily expected with France. The parliament took the safety of the king into consideration. His household was regulated and, in particular, it was ordered that no Frenchman or Welshman should remain about his person. The wisdom of this provision soon became very apparent. A league, offensive and defensive, was formed between Charles VII and Owain. Glyndŵr ratified this treaty on January 12th 1405 from his castle of Llanbadarn.

Fortune now began to frown upon Glyndŵr. He had still strength sufficient to keep within his mountainous territories but became too weak to meditate anything more than marauding invasions. Rhys Ddu and Philip Scudamore, two of Owain's best officers, he sent into Shropshire where they committed great excesses. They were both made prisoners, sent to London and executed. Glyndŵr maintained that extensive tract that forms the Alps of our country and kept his prisoners securely confined not far from his house, in the parish of Llansantffraid Glyndyfrdwy. The place is to this day called Carchardy Owain Glyndŵr.

Henry died in the beginning of 1413 and left his youthful successor so engaged in preparations for the conquest of France as to lose all thoughts of the entire subjection of his dominions in Britain. Glyndŵr remained still inaccessible but was so closely guarded as to cease to be tremendous. We find that Glyndŵr maintained his situation for 2 years longer. In 1415, his affairs bore so respectable an aspect that the king condescended to enter into a treaty with him. It is probable that it was interrupted by the death of our hero, which happened on September 20th 1415 in the 61st year of his age at the house of one of his daughters. Whether that of his daughter Scudamore or Monnington is uncertain but, according to the tradition of the county of Hereford, it may be supposed to have been at that of the last. It is said that he was buried in the church-yard of Monnington but there is no monument or any memorial of the spot that contains his remains.

Both the printed histories and the manuscript accounts represent his latter end to have been very miserable: that he wandered from place to place in the habit of a shepherd, in a low and forlorn condition, sheltering in caves and desert places from the fury of his enemies. This does not wear the face of probability for, had his situation been so deplorable, the king would never have condescended to propose terms to such a scourge as Glyndŵr had been to his kingdom. This retreat, and the distresses he underwent, were probably after the battle of Pwll Melyn in 1405, from which he quickly emerged. Death alone deprived Owain of the glory of accepting an offered accommodation. The treaty was renewed on February 24th 1416 with Maredudd ap Owain, the son of Glyndŵr, and peace was restored to England after an indecisive struggle of more than 15 years. Our chieftain died unsubdued, unfortunate only in foreseeing a second subjugation of his country after the loss of the great supporter of its independence.

Crossing the Dyfrdwy at Llangollen, I rode about a mile and turned a little out of the road in a fertile little vale. The abbey of Valle Crucis is solemnly seated on a small meadowy flat at the foot of the mountains, watered by a pretty stream and shaded with hanging woods. The valley in which the abbey stood was called, long prior to the foundation of the religious house, Pant y Groes or the Bottom of the Cross, doubtlessly from the ancient column erected in memory of Eliseg. This was a house of Cistercians, founded in the year 1200 by Madog ap Gruffudd Maelor, Lord of Bromfield and grandson by his mother's side to Owain Gwynedd Prince of Wales. I cannot discover any of the endowments further than half the tithes of Wrecsam, bestowed on it by Bishop Reyner of Llanelwy and, in 1127, his successor Bishop Abraham. The monks obtained the patronage of several other livings but their title to these was disputed by Bishop Anian, a Dominican, who brought his cause before the pope's delegates and obtained a decision in favour of him and his successors. As there was some doubt about the patronage of the church of Llandegla, they allotted (in lieu of it) to the abbey a third of the tithes of Bryn-Eglwys.

Two of the abbots, Dafydd ap Ieuan Iorwerth and Ioan or John, were highly celebrated by the bard Gutyn Owain who flourished about the year 1480. He highly commends their hospitality: speaks of their having 4 courses of meat, bright silver dishes, claret, et cetera. Gutyn does not forget the piety of the house and is particularly happy in being blessed by the abbot John with his 3 fingers covered with rings.

This house was dissolved in 1235 and is said to have been the first of the Welsh that underwent that fate. James I granted it to Edward Wotton, afterwards created Lord Wotton. There still remain the ruins of the church and part of the abbey, the last inhabited by a farmer. Much of the building is made of the coarse slaty stone of the country, the door and window frames of fine free-stone.

About a quarter of a mile higher up the vale, I met with the remainder of a round column, perhaps the most ancient of any British inscribed pillar now existing. It was entire till the civil wars of the last century when it was thrown down and broken by some ignorant fanatics who thought it had too much the appearance of a cross to be suffered to stand. The pillar had been a sepulchral cross; folly and superstition paid it the usual honours. It stood on a great tumulus, perhaps always environed with wood according to the custom of the most ancient times. It was dedicated to Concenn or Congen, the grandson of Brochmael Ysgithrog, the same who was defeated in 607 at the battle of Chester. The inscription is now illegible but, from the copy taken by Mr Edward Llwyd, the alphabet nearly resembles one of those used in the 6th century.

I returned by Valle Crucis and, after winding along a steep midway to the old castle, descended and, after crossing the rill of the Brân, arrived in the valley of Glisseg. One of the principal of the Glisseg rocks is honoured with the name of Craig-Arthur. That at the end of the vale is called Craig y Forwyn, or the maiden's; is bold, precipitous and terminates with a vast natural column. This valley is chiefly inhabited (happily) by an independent race of warm and wealthy yeomanry, undevoured as yet by the great men of the country.

The pass called Bwlch y Rhiw Felen is distinguished by the deaths of the 2 sons of the 6th century Cambrian prince Llywarch Hen. They were slain in battle and their loss deplored in an elegy by the princely bard, their father, of which these lines are a fragment:

*Bedd Guell yn y Rhiw Felen*
*Bedd Sawyl yn Llangollen*

*Pillar of Eliseg*

Guell found a grave in Rhiw Felen,
Sawyl in Llangollen.

Llywarch Hen left his country to expel the Saxons out of this part of Britain. He leaves us ignorant of the event. All he acquaints us with is that he lost twelve sons in the generous attempt.

Tomen y Rhodwydd was once a fortress known by the name of the castle of Yale, built by Owain Gwynedd about the year 1148. It consists of a vast artificial mount with another still loftier near one end, the keep of the place. We are told that this short-lived castelet was burnt by Iorwerth Goch ap Maredudd 9 years after its erection. It is in this manner that we must account for the total disappearance of many Welsh castles whose names are preserved in history and whose vestiges we have sought for in vain. They were made of wood as was very customary with several ancient nations and with others of later date.

I crossed the country for about 2 miles to the village of Llandegla, noted for its vast fairs for black cattle. The church is dedicated to St Tegla, virgin and martyr who, after her conversion by St Paul, suffered under Nero at Iconium. A small spring rises about 200 yards from the church. The water is to this day held to be extremely beneficial in the Clwyf Tegla (*St Tegla's disease*) or the falling sickness. The patient washes his limbs in the well, makes an offering into it of 4 pence, walks round it 3 times and thrice repeats the Lord's prayer. The votary then enters the church, gets under the communion table, lies down with the Bible under his head, is covered with a carpet or cloth, and rests there till the break of day, departing after offering 6 pence and leaving a fowl in the church. If the bird dies, the cure is supposed to have been effected and the disease transferred to the devoted victim.

# Chapter Five

# Yr Wyddgrug to Caerwys to Downing

**I CONTINUED** my journey to Llanarmon, a village whose church is dedicated to St Germanus, Bishop of Auxerre, who, with St Lupus, contributed to gain the famous Victoria Alleluiatica over the Picts and Saxons near Yr Wyddgrug. In Leland's days, there was a great resort of pilgrims and large offerings at this place, and probably to an image of an ecclesiastic still to be seen in the church-wall.

Sepulchral tumuli are very frequent in this parish. I was present at the opening of one, composed of loose stones and earth covered with a layer of soil about 2 feet thick, and over that a coat of verdant turf. Several urns made of sub-burnt clay were discovered, of a reddish colour on the outside, stained black within by the ashes they contained. The custom of burning the remains of the dead ceased with paganism. It therefore fell first into disuse with the Welsh for it was some time retained by the Saxons after their conquest of this kingdom but was left off on their receiving the light of the gospel.

Upon the bank of the river, near the village of Llanarmon Dyffryn Ceiriog, is a vast artificial mount called Tomen y Fardra, once the site of a castelet, the relics of which appear in a small square foundation. The river bounds one side of the mount, a deep ditch the other. Not far from it is a great natural cavern of a considerable height, for some space; it then lowers and extends to an unknown length.

From Llanarmon I continued my journey along the bad roads of that parish. The country grows more contracted by the approximation of the hills. On one side are the rocky ledges of limestone, rich in lead-ore, and on the left are the Clwydian hills which divide this country from the vale of Clwyd.

Moel Fenlli, or Benlli's hill, is remarkable for having on it a strong British post, guarded as usual by dikes and fosses. This probably was possessed by a chieftain of that name for Nennius speaks of such a regulus of the country of Yale. As too usual with our ancient historians, Nennius blends so ridiculous a legend with the mention of him as would destroy belief of his existence did not the hill remain a possible evidence.

I continued eastward along the great road into Y Fflint. This was anciently inhabited by a hardy race at perpetual feud with the men of Cheshire on one side and the men of Yale on the other. My countrymen never suffered their active swords to rust; in default of Saxon, they would take up with the blood of their Cambrian neighbours.

Yr Wyddgrug consists principally of one broad and handsome street on a gentle rising in the midst of a small but rich plain. The church is placed on an eminence and is of the time of Henry VII. At the north end of the town stands the mount to which it owes the Celtic and Latin names, Yr Wyddgrug and Mons Altus, the lofty or conspicuous mount.

Much of the country was so covered with woods that Edward, before his conquest of Wales, was obliged to cut a passage through them in the tract between Yr Wyddgrug and a place called Swerdewood, and to direct that nothing should be required for the damage done to the owners. I find he called in a number of cutters for this purpose and, in the next year, not fewer than 200 cutters and colliers (carbonarii) who were summoned out of the forest of Dean and the county of Hereford.

From Yr Wyddgrug I took the west side of the vale, a tract filled with numbers of gentlemen's seats of independent fortunes, as yet not caught and absorbed in the gulfy vortex of our Leviathans. These are the remnants of the custom of gavelkind so prevalent formerly in North Wales.

Abundance of limestone is burnt into lime on Caergwrle hill, a lofty mountain composed of that species of stone, from which a vast trade is carried into Cheshire. Near the top are found, in loose earth, numbers of the bodies called entrochi, of a curious and uncommon sort with round protuberant joints. Fossilists suppose them to have been parts of some species of arborescent sea-star whose branches bear a resemblance to these substances. In former times, millstones were cut out of the rock on which the castle stands, which is composed of small pebbles lodged in grit.

On Rhuthun demesne, belonging to Sir Stephen Glynne, adjoining to the Alun, are 2 springs strongly impregnated with salt which, in dry weather, used to be a great resort of pigeons to pick up the hardened particles. These were formerly resorted to as a remedy in scorbutic cases. The patients drank a quart or 2 in a day, and some boiled the water till half was wasted before they took it. The effect was purging, griping and sickness at the stomach, which went off in a few days and then produced a good appetite. Dr Short gives an instance of a woman in a deplorable condition from a deep scurvy, who was perfectly restored by the use of these springs.

From the village of Estyn, I returned on the north side of the valley, repassed Yr Wyddgrug and, about a mile west of the town, visited Maes Garmon, a spot that still retains the name of the saintly commander in the celebrated battle fought in 420 between the Welsh, headed by the bishops Germanus and Lupus, and a crowd of pagan Picts and Saxons who were carrying desolation through the country. This event happened in Easter week when the Christian army, wet with their recent baptism in the river Alun, were led by their holy commanders against the pagan host. Germanus instructed them to attend to the word he gave and repeat it. Accordingly he pronounced that of Alleluia. His soldiers caught the sacred sound and repeated it with such ecstatic force that, the hills resounding with the cry, struck terror into the enemy who fled on all sides; numbers perished by the sword and numbers in the adjacent river.

Such is the relation given by Constantius of Lyons who wrote the life of St Germanus within 32 years after the death of the saint. It has been objected by cavillers that the Saxons were not at that time possessed of Britain. That may be admitted but the learned Usher overthrows the objection by rightly observing that those people had long before made temporary invasions to our island and committed great ravages in several parts.

I proceeded towards Cilcain and saw in my way Hesb-Alun, (the dry Alun), where the river sinks under the ground like the sullen mole and continues a subterraneous course for half a mile before emerging to the day. In this parish, on the side of the turnpike road, not far from Cilcain hall, is the noted Ffynnon Leinw (Flowing Well), a large oblong well with a double wall round it. This is taken notice of by Camden for its flux and reflux but the singularity has ceased since his time, according to the best information I can receive. Cilcain hall is a seat of a branch of the Mostyns, now the property of Mr Edwards of Pentre in Trefaldwyn, in right of his first wife Charlotte Mostyn, heiress of the place.

Penbedw is seated in a manor of the same name, granted July 17th 1544 by Henry VIII to Peter (Pyers) ap Hywel, alias Peter Mostyn, of Wespre, in consideration of the payment of 73 pounds in hand. In the meadows below the house is part of a druidical circle and a small tumulus. On one of the summits of the mountain, at a great height above the house, is a very strong British post called Moel Arthur, probably in honour of our celebrated prince. This is one of the chain of posts that defended the country of the Ordovices, and their successors, against the inroads of invaders. They were occasionally made use of in after times, even in the time of Owain Glyndŵr. They are generally destitute of water, which evinces that they were intended merely as temporary retreats for families, herds and flocks, on a sudden invasion. The fighting men kept to the field while all that was dear and valuable was committed under a proper garrison. They are always placed within sight of one another so that, by fires or other signals, notice might be given of the approach of an enemy. This chain is formed by Moel Hiraddug in the parish of Cwm, Copa'r Goleuni *(Mount of Light)* above Trelawnyd, Moel y Gaer in the parish of Bodfari, Bryn y Cloddiau *(the hill of ditches)*, Moel Arthur, Moel y Crio on Halkin mountain, Moel Fennli and another Moel y Gaer. I could give a long list of these posts, perhaps as far as the Severn sea and the trans-Sabrine parts of the Cornavii, but these suffice for the present purpose.

Soon after passing Penbedw, I reached Nannerch, a hamlet with a small church. This valley is a boundary of the mineral tract of our county, limestone forming one side of the narrow value of Nannerch, and shattery slaty stone composing the other. The ore of lead has been followed to the depth of a 130 or 140 yards with an unprofitable vein appearing below. The veins run either north and south or east and west but the lead got in the first scarcely ever produces a quantity of silver worth the refiner's labour. The minerals of the tracts in question are ore of lead, calamine and zinc (called by the miners 'black jack'). The upper part of a vein of lead ore is always richest in silver; the bottom in lead. Our refiners will assay any lead that will yield 10 ounces in the ton of lead and upwards. The usual produce is 14 ounces; 16 have been gotten but acquisitions of that kind within this circuit are extremely uncommon.

We have had at different periods mines productive of vast wealth in several parts of this tract. The richest vein was discovered about 50 years ago at Rowley's rake or Pant y Pwll dŵr on Halkin mountain which, in less than 3 years, yielded to different proprietors, adventurers and smelters above a million in money. It is at this time an undetermined question whether more wealth has been gotten out of the earth or more lost in the search after prizes in this subterraneous lottery.

Petroleum, or rock-oil, is sometimes found in crevices of the mines. It has an agreeable smell and is esteemed serviceable in rheumatic cases if rubbed on the parts affected. The miners call it *Ymenyn tylwyth* (the fairies' butter). Perhaps these fairies are the same as those (in superstitious days called knockers) which, by repeated strokes, were believed to direct the miners to a rich vein. But in fact the noises often heard in mines are always discovered to proceed from the dropping of water.

From Nannerch, I continued my journey along the narrow vale, picturesquely ornamented with hanging woods. Leave the church of Ysgeifiog on the right. In the parish was shot, a few years ago, that singular bird the Hoopoe (volume 1 number 90 of *British Zoology*). This species is easily distinguishable by its large crest, long slender incurvated bill, and by having only 10 feathers in the tail.

At the junction of the vales of Nannerch and Bodfari, I ascended to Caerwys, a town mouldering away with age. It consists of 4 streets crossing each other at right angles answering to the 4 points of the compass. The name, as Camden has long since observed, savours of great antiquity: Caer, the fortress, and Gwŷs, a summons. Caerwys, with a neighbouring town called Tref Edwyn (now lost), and Rhuddlan, had been from very early time the seats of the judicature for these parts of Wales. In Caerwys were held the great sessions. It had its town-hall and its jail and was the place of execution. It remained the place of judicature till sometime past the middle of the last century when the courts were removed to Y Fflint.

In the 26th year of Henry III, 1241, that prince granted to the inhabitants a charter exempting them from the amobr but at the same time imposed on them an obligation to find 24 people who were to keep the peace of the country. This town, Picton, Axton and other hamlets were to find 3 men each to work 3 days in the harvest as they were wont in the days of the 2 preceding Welsh princes.

Caerwys has the most considerable fairs for cattle, sheep and horses in all the county. The first John Trevor, Bishop of Llanelwy, appears among the subscribers to a charter for a market in 1356 but the markets have now failed entirely since the increase of Treffynnon.

What gave a particular glory to the town of Caerwys was the honour it had of being the place of the Eisteddfod, the sessions of the bards and minstrels, for many centuries. It was the resort of those of a certain district, as Aberffro in Ynys Môn was of those of that island and the neighbouring county, and Mathrafal of those of the land of Powys. The two last were the residence of princes and Caerwys the residence of Llywelyn ap Gruffudd.

These Eisteddfods were the Welsh Olympics. Fired at first with generous emulation, our poets crowded into the list and carried off the prize, contented with the mere honour of victory. At length, when the competitors became more numerous and the country became oppressed with the multitude, new regulations of course took place. The disappointed candidates were no longer suffered to torture the ears of the principality with their wretched compositions. None but bards of merit were suffered to rehearse their pieces, and minstrels of skill to perform. These went through a long probation; judges were appointed to decide on their respective abilities, and degrees suitable were conferred with permissions for exercising their talents. The judges were appointed by commission from our princes and, after the conquest of Wales, by the kings of England.

Edward I exercised a political cruelty over the generation of bards of his time yet future princes thought fit to revive an institution so likely to soften the manners of a fierce people. The crown had the power of nominating the judges, who decided not only on the merit but the subject of the poems. Like our lord chamberlains, they were certain of licensing only those which were agreeable to the English court.

The Bardi (the 'Beirdd' of the Welsh) were of great authority among the Celtic nations: The Germans were animated in battle by verses delivered in a deep and solemn tone. Among the Gauls, bards sang the actions of great men and particularly celebrated in their hymns the heroes who fell in fight.

It is highly probable that the bards and minstrels were under certain regulations during the time of Druidism but we find no proofs of them till long after, in the days of Cadwaladr (last King of Britain, who died at Rome about the year 688). Of him it is said that, being at an assembly of this nature with his nobles, there came a minstrel and played in a key so displeasing that he and all his brethren were prohibited, under a severe penalty, from ever playing on it any more, but were ordered to adopt that of Mwynen Gwynedd or the sweet key of Gwynedd.

I imagine that there had been musical regulations in Britain previous to this. I find from Mr Morris's manuscripts of British music that a tune called Gosteg yr Halen, or the Prelude of the Salt, was always played whenever the salt-seller was placed before King Arthur's knights at his round table.

After Cadwaladr, the next princes who undertook the reform of our minstrelsy were Bleddyn ap Cynfyn and Gruffudd ap Cynan. The first was contemporary with the conqueror; the last with King Stephen. These enacted that no person should follow the profession of bard or minstrel but such only who were admitted by the Eisteddfod, which was held once in 3 years. They were prohibited from invading one another's province nor were they permitted to degrade themselves by following any other occupation. Neither bard nor minstrel was to demand above 10 shillings in any article, under pain of losing the whole besides being suspended from their profession for 3 years.

After the times of the princes, the great men, their descendants, took these people under their care and protection, allowing them the liberty of circuiting their respective territories at Christmas, Easter and Whitsuntide, and the whole principality once in 3 years.

The bards were held in the highest repute. I cannot give a stronger idea of the esteem they were in than by citing from the Welsh Laws the account of their rank in the prince's court and the various rewards and fees they were entitled to, and the severe penalties that were enacted to preserve their persons from insult. They were supposed to be endowed with powers equal to inspiration. They were the oral historians of all past transactions, public and private. They related the great events of the state and, like the scalds of the northern nations, retained the memory of numberless transactions which otherwise would have perished in oblivion. They were likewise thoroughly acquainted with the words of the 3 primary bards: Myrddin ap Morfryn, Myrddin Emrys and Taliesin ben Beirdd. But they had another talent which probably endeared them more than all the rest to the Welsh nobility: that of being most accomplished genealogists and in singing the deeds of an ancestry derived from the most distance period.

The Bardd Teulu, or Court Bard, held the 8th place in the prince's court. He possessed his land free. The prince supplied him with a horse and woollen robe and the princess with linen. He sat next to the governor of the palace at the 3 great festivals for, at those seasons, the governor was to deliver him his harp. On the same festivals he was also to have the Disdain's, or steward of the household's, garment for his fee.

When a song is called for, the Cadeir-fardd, or the bard who has got the Badge of the Chair, is first to sing a hymn in glory of God; after that, another in honour of the prince. When those are over, the Teuluwr or Bard of the Hall is to sing some other subject.

If the princess calls for a song after she has retired from table to her apartment, the Teulu must sing to her highness in a low voice lest he should disturb the performers in the hall. John Dafydd Rhys says that the subject was to be on death but I rather follow Wotton who, instead of angau which signifies death, prefers the word amgen or a separate subject from what was sung in the hall.

When the bard goes with the prince's servants on a plundering expedition and performs before them his animating compositions, he is to have the finest heifer of the booty. In case the detachment was drawn up in order of battle, he was to sing at their head the praises of the Welsh monarchy. This was to remind them of their ancient right to the whole kingdom. Their inroads being almost always on the English territories, they thought they did no more than seize on their own.

The prince bestowed on him an ivory chess-board (others say a harp) and the princess a golden ring. His lodging was to be with the governor of the palace.

When he is required to sing with other bards, by way of distinction he is to have a double portion.

If the bard asks any favour of the prince, he must sing one of his compositions; if of a nobleman, 3; if of a common person, he must sing till he is so weary as to rest on his elbow or to fall asleep. This, I fear, shows our bards were a very importuning race and required check; yet still they were in high estimation. Their gwerth, or compensation for their life, was rated at 126 cows, and any injury done them at 6 cows and 120 pence.

The Merch-Gobr of his daughter or marriage fine of his daughter was 120 pence. Her cowyll, argyffreu, or nuptial presents, was 30 shillings, and her portion 3 pounds. It is remarkable that the Pencerdd Gwlad or chief of the faculty was entitled to the merch-gobr or amobr for the daughters of all the inferiors of the faculty within the district who paid 24 pence on their marriage; which not only shows the antiquity but the great authority of these people.

The Pencerdd was not among the officers of the court but occasionally sat in the tenth place. He also had his land free, was to perform much in the same manner as the court bard, whom he seems to have taken place of whenever he attended. When the Pencerdd was present, the former sat only in the 12th seat. No other was to play without license from him. The chief musicians were each to receive from their lord the first a harp, the second a crwth, the third a pipe which, on their deaths, were to revert to the lord.

The prince's harp was valued at 120 pence and that of Pencerdd at the same; the key at 24 pence; a gentleman's harp was estimated at 60 pence.

It must be observed that players on crwths with 3 strings, taborers and pipers were reckoned among the ignoble performers; they were not allowed to sit down and had only a penny for their pains.

There were 4 degrees in the poetical faculty:

Y Disgybl Yspâs, or the lowest disciple, was obliged to understand the construction of the 5 species of Englyn and to compose them before a Pencerdd, who was to declare upon his conscience that the candidate was endowed with a true poetical genius.

After this he commenced Disgybl Disgyblaidd. Here he becomes a graduate but must understand 12 of our different metres and produce specimens of each, of his own composition. If in 3 years time he does not merit the next degree, he is degraded from this.

If successful, he proceeds to the degree of Disgybl Penceirddiaidd or candidate for degree of Pencerdd when he must understand the propriety of expressions and the different metres and compose in 21 species. If in 3 years he does not attain by his own merit to the next degree, he falls back into that of Disgybl Disgyblaidd.

Otherwise he becomes a Penbardd or Pencerdd, chief of the faculty he was candidate in, when it is necessary he should be accomplished in every branch of his art. He then received the badge of the silver harp, or that of a golden or silver chair, which he wore upon his shoulder. He was also placed with much ceremony on a magnificent chair, part of the furniture mentioned in the patent. A Pencerdd might challenge any other to rehearse or sing for the prize after giving a year and a day's notice. If he succeeded, he carried it off; if not, he lost his degree and the victor kept the prize for life but was obliged to produce it annually on the Eisteddfod.

In instrumental music, there were 5 degrees, differing nothing from those in the other faculty except in the 2 lowest:

1. The Disgybl yspas heb râdd, or without a degree.
2. Disgybl yspas graddawl, or graduated.
3. Disgybl dyscyblaidd.
4. Disgybl penceirddiaidd.
5. Pencerdd.

These, like the others, were to be attained by their respective merits in the science but, as their qualifications are expressed in technical terms of Welsh music, it is past my skill to give an explanation. None but a Pencerdd should presume to become an instructor. The chief of our days was that uncommon genius, the blind Mr John Parry, late of Ruabon, who had the kingdom for his Clych clera (musical circuit) and remained unrivalled.

Our Pencerdds, once qualified, were licensed to sing or to perform under certain restrictions. By the law of our princes, particular regard was paid to their morals: "They were to be no make-bates, no vagabonds, no ale-house haunters, no drunkards, no brawlers, no whore-hunters, no thieves, nor companions of such. If they offend, every man, by the statute, is made an officer and authorised to arrest and punish them and to take all that they have about them".

The bards of those times often accompanied their voices with the harp, as they were wont of old, in the manner described by Ammianus Marcellinus. There was also another species of musician, of an inferior kind, called Datceiniad, who accompanied the musical instruments of others with his song.

The most inferior of the musical tribe was the Datceiniad pen pastwyn (he that sang to the beating of his club), being ignorant of every other kind of instrument. If there was a professor of music present, his leave must first be obtained before he presumed to entertain the company with this species of melody.

# Chapter Six

# The Journey to Snowdon, 1786

**IN THIS,** the sequel of my former tour, I directed my course westward from Downing, passed by Whitford, our parish-church, and ascended the hill of Garreg (The Rock), a high and most conspicuous part of the country. The Romans took advantage of Garreg and placed on its summit a Pharos to conduct the navigators to and from Deva along the difficult channel of the Seteia Portus. The building is still remaining. I hope my friends will not deem me an antiquarian Quixote and imagine me mistaking a building hitherto supposed to have been a windmill for a Roman lighthouse. Withinside are the vestiges of a staircase which led to the floors, of which there appear to have been 2. Along the upper floor are 8 openings in which were placed the lights which the Romans thought necessary to keep distinct lest they should be mistaken by seamen for a star.

About a mile from hence, visit the small town of Trelawnyd, almost the entire creation of its then owner, John Wynne of Gop, who died in the present century. The ancient name of the parish is Trelawnyd for which I can find no satisfactory reason. Here is fixed one of the charity-schools, founded and opened in 1726 by doctor Daniel Williams, a dissenting minister, with an endowment of 8 pounds a year; a charity which he extended to every county in North Wales, distinguishing that at Wrecsam, the place of his birth, by an annual salary of 15 pounds. He also established a fund, I believe, to each, from which children are apprenticed at 5 pounds apiece.

From the town I ascended the hill called Copa'r Goleuni, on whose summit is a most enormous carnedd or tumulus formed of lime-stones. It was probably the site of a specula or exploratory tower and memorial of some chieftain. The tract from hence to Caerwys was certainly a field of battle; no place in North Wales exhibits an equal quantity of tumuli. It will not be too hazardous a conjecture to suppose that in this place was the slaughter of the Ordovices by Agricola. Part of the brow of the hill is called Bryn y Saethau or the Hill of the Arrows, from being the station of the archers in the engagement.

Descend to the church and village of Llanasa, the former dedicated to St Asaph. In my approach from these high lands towards the shore, observe the ruins of a small chapel at the little hamlet of Gwesbyr near Talacre, one of the seats of Sir Pyers Mostyn. His adjacent quarry is noted for the excellence of the free-stone; and his vast and profitable warren beneath noted for the delicacy of the rabbits by reason of their feeding on the maritime plants.

Pass over Gronant-Moor. There is a tradition that its extent was so great that the people on this side could hold conversation over the channel with those of Cheshire. It appears that this flat was formerly very extensive and was reduced to its present scanty limits by the fury of the sea. In the church-yard wall of Abergele is a dateless epitaph in Welsh signifying that the person interred there lived 3 miles to the north of that spot, a tract now entirely possessed by the sea.

On approaching Prestatyn, about 2 miles from Trelacre, the flat becomes extremely fertile in corn, especially wheat. The road from hence to Dyserth is extremely pleasant. The white rock makes a conspicuous figure on the left, and its sides appeared deeply trenched by the miners in search of ore. The church of Dyserth, overshaded with great yews, forms a most striking appearance. A water-fall in the deep and rounded hollow of a rock once gave additional beauty to this spot but of late the diverting of the waters to a mill has robbed the place of this elegant variation. The stream flows from Fynnon Asaph, St Asaph's Well, in a dingle in the parish of Cwm about a mile distant. The fountain is inclosed with stone, in a polygonal form, and had formerly its votaries like that of St Winefrede.

Above Dyserth church, on a high rock, stand the remains of its castle which went by the names of Din-colyn, Castell y Ffailon and Castell Gerri. It was probably Welsh and last in the chain of British posts on the Clwydian hills. Henry II fortified it in 1241 but its date was short for in 1261 Llywelyn ap Gruffudd raised both this castle and that of Deganwy. The fragments of the castle lie in vast masses, overthrown by mining which was a common method of besieging before the use of powder.

Moel Hiraddug, a Celtic post on a very steep and rocky hill, stands to the south of the castle and forms the next to it in the chain of fortresses. On the summit of the hill is a great bed of beautiful red spar which seems to take its tinge from iron ore, dug probably in the time of the Saxons.

The small borough of Rhuddlan is seated high on the red clayey banks of the Clwyd above Morfa-Rhuddlan, a marsh celebrated for the battle in 795 between the Saxons and Welsh. Our monarch Caradog fell in the conflict. We say that Offa, the famous King of Mercia, was slain here but the Saxon Chronicle places his death the year before that battle.

The castle had been a handsome building. Edward I made it the great magazine of provision for the support of his army in its advance into the country. The reigning prince, Llywelyn ap Gruffudd, knew the danger of leaving so consequential a place in the hands of his enemy but it resisted all the most vigorous efforts made on it in 1281 by Llywelyn and his brother Dafydd who had become reconciled by their common danger. Soon after, it proved the place of Dafydd's confinement not long before his ignominious end at Shrewsbury.

A piece of ancient building, called the Parliament House, is still to be seen in Rhuddlan. From hence he actually practised the well-known deceit of giving the Welsh a prince born among them, who never spoke a word of English and whose life and conversation no man was able to stain; all of which our discontented nobility eagerly accepted, little thinking the person intended was the infant Edward just born at Caernarfon.

Fording the Clwyd, I soon came in sight of Llanelwy. The handsome extensive bridge, the little town and the cathedral, mixed with trees, form a most agreeable view. When Kentigern, Bishop of Glasgow, was driven from his see in 542, he retired into Wales and established here a monastery for 965 monks, instituted on the same plan with that of Bangor; part for labour, part for prayer. Here he built a church and, having won over the Welsh prince Maglocunus, once his violent opponent, established here a see and was himself the first bishop. Being recalled to Scotland, he nominated for successor Asaph or Hassaph, a Briton of great piety and good family (grandson of Pabo post Prydain). He died in 596, was buried in his cathedral and gave name to the place.

At Llannerch, the chief seat of my kinsman the late John Davies, about half a mile to the east of the bridge, I stopped a while to admire the charming view of the vale of Clwyd with the magnificent boundary between it and Fflint. From Tremeirchion green, placed high above Llannerch, is a very fine view of the whole vale, of the western boundary, and the lofty tract of Yr Wyddfa. In Tremeirchion church is the mutilated tomb of Sir Robert Pounderling. By his crossed legs it seems he had attained the merit of pilgrimage to the holy sepulchre.

Cross the Clwyd on Pont y Cambwell and, turning to the left, cross it again at Pont Gruffudd in order to search in the parish of Bodfari for the ancient Varis. Soon enter the deep pass formed by nature in the Clwydian hills, from the vales of Fflint. The sole remaining antiquity is Celtic, a post on a hill to the left called Moel y Gaer (*Hill of the Camp*). Llywelyn ap Gruffudd, last Prince of Wales, resided at Llys Maes Mynan whose foundations, till within these few years, were to be seen in an adjacent meadow.

Quit the turnpike road on the left, ford the Wheeler and, after crossing the Clwyd, reach Llyweni hall. On this spot is said to have resided, about the year 720, Marchweithian, one of the 15 tribes or nobility of northern Wales. Sir John Salisbury the Strong succeeded to the estate on the execution of his elder brother Thomas, who suffered in 1586 for his concern in Babington's plot.

Catherine Tudur, better known as Catherine of Berain, is exceedingly celebrated in this part of Wales. She was the daughter and heiress of Tudur ap Robert Fychan of Berain; she took for her first husband John Salisbury, heir of Llyweni, and on his death gave her hand to Sir Richard Clough. The tradition goes that, at the funeral of her spouse, she was led to the church by Sir Richard and from church to church by Morris Wynne of Gwydir who whispered to her his wish of being her second. She refused him with great civility, informing him that she had accepted the proposals of Sir Richard in her way to church; but she assured him that, in case she performed the same sad duty to the knight, he might depend on being the third. She concluded with a 4th husband, Edward Thelwal of Plas y Ward before departing this life August 27th 1591.

The chief of Mr Fitzmaurice's improvements is a bleachery of uncommon extent. The building is in the form of a crescent: a beautiful arcade 400 feet in extent. The greatest part of the linen bleached here is sent from the tenantry of his great estates in Ireland in payment of rent. Much also is sent by private persons from the neighbouring counties for the mere purpose of whitening.

Dafydd, brother of our last Llywelyn, makes great complaints of the havoc made by Reginald de Grey, justice of Chester, in cutting down his wood of Lleweni which Dafydd probably held as Lord of Dinbych.

In the church of Whitchurch, or St Marcellus, a small brass shows Richard Middleton, governor of Denbigh castle under Edward VI. Behind him are 9 sons and behind his wife Jane are 7 daughters. Several of the sons were men of distinguished characters. The 6th son, Hugh, was a person whose useful life would give lustre to the greatest family. This gentleman (afterwards Sir Hugh) began, as we are told by himself, searching for coal within a mile of his native place. He planned and brought to perfection the great design of supplying London with water.

This plan was meditated in the reign of Elizabeth but no one was found bold enough to attempt it. In 1608, the dauntless Welshman stepped forth and Smote the Rock and on Michelmas 1613 the waters flowed into the thirsting metropolis. He brought it, in defiance of hills and valleys, nearly 39 miles.

Two thousand pounds a month which he gained from the Ceredigion mines were swallowed up in this river. He received the empty honour of seeing himself attended by the king, his court and all the corporation of London, among whom was his brother (designed mayor for the ensuing year). The waters gushed out in their presence and the great architect received their applause, a knighthood and in 1622 the title of baronet. His own fair fortune being expended on an undertaking which now brings the proprietors an amazing revenue, he was reduced to become a hireling surveyor and was eminently useful in every place where draining or mining was requisite. I shall have occasion to speak of some of his labours in the course of this book.

A mural monument needlessly attempts to preserve the memory of that great antiquary, Humphrey Llwyd. He is represented in Spanish dress, kneeling at an altar, beneath a range of small arches; above, a multitude of quarterings proclaim his long descent. After the panegyric passed on him by Camden, it would be presumptuous to add any thing relative to his great skill in the antiquities of our country. He practised, for his amusement, physic and music.

A little further stands Dinbych, placed, like Stirling, on the slope of a great rock crowned with a castle. Its ancient Welsh name was Castell Caledfryn yn Rhos, the former name of the tract in which it is seated. The word Dinbych, the present Welsh appellation, signifies a small hill which it is comparative to the neighbouring mountains. The first time I find any reference to it is in the beginning of the reign of Edward I from whom Dafydd, in defiance of his brother Llywelyn, chose to hold his lordship together with the cantred of Dyffryn Clwyd. He made it his residence till the conquest of our country, soon after which he was taken near the place and carried, loaded with irons, to the English monarch at Rhuddlan.

The castle crowns the summit of the hill, one side of which is quite precipitous. Leland relates a particular of this fortress which I do not find in any other historian; he says that Edward IV was besieged in it and that he was permitted to retire on condition that he quit the kingdom for ever.

The present town covers great part of the slope of the hill and some streets extend along the plain. Its manufactures in shoes and gloves are very considerable and great quantities are annually sent to London for its warehouses and for exportation.

Having made Gwaenynog my headquarters for this neighbourhood, I one day visited from thence Henllan, the parish church of these parts, remarkable for the schism between church and steeple, the first having retreated into the bottom while the last maintains its station of the top of the hill. The church is covered with shingles, a species of roof almost obsolete. St Sadwrn or St Saturnus, contemporary with St Wenefrede, has it under his protection.

After a ride of a few miles, I reached Dyffryn Aled (*Vale of the River Aled*), a very narrow tract bounded by high hills. I descended a very steep wooded dell in the township of Penared to visit the gloomy cataract of Llyn yr Ogo where the Aled tumbles into a horrible black cavern overshaded by oaks. Somewhat higher up is another, exposed to the full day, falling from a vast height and dividing the naked glen. Llyn Aled, the small lake from which the river flows, lies at a small distance amidst black and healthy mountains through which runs much of the road to Gwytherin.

In my return, I followed the course of the Elwy by the church and village of Llangernyw, the seat of Robert Wynn. In this parish, above the Elwy, was one of the residences of Hedd Molwynog, descended from Rhodri Mawr, King of all Wales. A large mote called Yr Henllys marks the place. Molwynog was chief of one of the 15 tribes of northern Wales. He was contemporary with Dafydd ap Owain Gwynedd and assisted that prince to carry fire and sword through England, even to the walls of Coventry. I hope my countrymen will not grow indignant when I express my fears that in very early times we were as fierce and savage as the rest of Europe. They will bear this the better when they realise that they keep pace with it in civilisation and in the progress of every fine art. We cannot deny that we were, to the excess, "Jealous in honour, sudden and quick in quarrel".

Two gentlemen of this house exemplify the assertion. Meurig ap Bleddyn, resentful of the injuries which he and his tenants received from the English judges and officers, slew one of the first and hanged several of the latter on the oaks of his woods, by which he forfeited to the crown his lands. Bleddyn Fychan, another of this race, fell out with his tenants and in a fit of fury chased them from his estate and turned it into a forest; a pretty picture of the manners of the times!

Near the road to Ruthun is Bachymbyd, a seat and estate belonging to Lord Bagot. Near the side of the road are to be seen some very fine chestnut trees, one of which is near 24 feet in circumference. We are indebted for this species of tree to the Romans who probably first planted it in Kent.

Reach Ruthun and enter Porth y Dŵr, its only remaining gate. The town is pleasantly situated on the easy slope and summit of a rising ground. The castle stood on the south side and in part sunk beneath the earth. The views from the summit of the ruins are very well worthy of the traveller's attention. If he is fond of a more aerial one, I would be all means have him ascend the heights of Bwlch pen y Barras, from whence is a full prospect of our boasted vale and the remote hills of our Alpine tract. The Welsh name of the fortress is Castell Coch yn Gwernfor .

The town of Ruthun was burnt by Owain Glyndŵr on September 20th 1400. He took the opportunity of surprising it during the fair, enriched his followers with the plunder and then retired to his fastnesses among the hills. In the last century, the castle was garrisoned by the loyalists and sustained, in 1646, a siege from February to the middle of April, when it surrendered with 2 months' provisions to general Mytton. The fortress was afterwards demolished. Doctor Gabriel Goodman, dean of Westminster in the time of Queen Elizabeth, was a native of Ruthun. His affection to learned men is evident by his establishing a free school for this parish and being the patron of the great Camden whom he enabled to take those travels which produced the finest collection of provincial antiquities ever extant.

The new jail does much honour to the architect, Mr Joseph Turner, comprehending all the requisites of these seats of misery: security, cleanness and health. The debtors are separated from the criminals by a very lofty wall dividing their respective yards which are very airy and spacious. The condemned cells are on a level with the ground, dry, light and strong; an excellent contrast to the sad dungeons of ancient prisons.

From Ruthun I visited the neat little mother church of Llan-rudd, dedicated to St Meuzan, a great astrologer and physician to King Gwrtheyrn (*Vortigern*). In it is the monument of John Thelwall of Bathafarn, and his wife, kneeling at an altar; behind him are 10 sons and behind her are 4 daughters. Of the sons, Sir Bevis is armed, the rest are in gowns, and 3 carry in their hands a skull to denote their early departure. Sir Bevis bought from one Gibbs a share of certain lands which were to be recovered from the sea at Brading-haven in the Isle of Wight. He admitted as partner his countryman, the famous Sir Hugh Middleton. Sir Hugh procured a number of Dutchmen to enclose and recover the haven from the sea but, after expending 7,000 pounds, Sir Bevis and he were obliged to retire and submit to their loss. The other 7 sons lived to advanced life and flourished cotemporaries in the several professions they had embraced.

Go over part of Coed Matchan, a large naked common noted for a quarry of coarse red and white marble. Descend into the narrow vale of Nant-clwyd and for some time ride over dreary commons. On one is a small encampment with a single fosse called Caer Senial. Near this place enter Meirionnydd. Within sight of the former, visit Caer Drewyn, another post, in full view of the beautiful vales of Glyndyfrdwy and Edeirnion, watered by the Dyfrdwy.

Pass by the house of Rug, memorable for the treacherous surprisal of Gruffudd ap Cynan, King of Wales, soon after his victory at Carno in the year 1077, having been inveigled hither by the treason of one Meirion Goch. Notwithstanding his eminent success he fell into a long captivity, being betrayed into the hands of Hugh Lupus Earl of Chester and Hugh Belesme Earl of Shrewsbury and was conveyed to the castle of Chester where he endured 12 years of imprisonment. At length he was released by the bravery of a young man of these parts, Cynwrig Hir. Coming to Chester under pretence of buying necessaries, Cynwrig took an opportunity, while the keepers were a feasting, to carry away his prince, loaden with irons, on his back, to a place of security.

Cross the Dyfrdwy on a very handsome bridge of 6 arches and reach Corwen whose church and small town, seated beneath a vast rock at the foot of the Berwyn hills, form a picturesque view from various parts of the preceding ride. Corwen is celebrated for being the great rendezvous of the Welsh forces under Owain Gwynedd who from hence put a stop to the invasion of Henry II in the year 1165. The place of encampment is marked, as I am told, by a rampart of earth above the church southward and by the marks of abundance of tents from thence to the village of Cynwyd.

The vast Berwyn mountains are the eastern boundary of this beautiful vale. Their highest tops are the Cader Fronwen (*White Breast*) and Cader Ferwyn. On the first is a great heap of stones brought from some distant part, with great toil, up the steep ascent, and in their middle is an erect pillar. Of him whose ambition climbed this height for a monument we are left in ignorance. Under the summit is said to run an artificial road called Ffordd Helen, or Helen's Way; a lady of whose labours I shall soon have occasion to speak further. On these hills is found the Rubus Chamaemorus (*Cloud Berries or Knot Berries*). The Swedes and Norwegians reckon the berries to be excellent antiscorbutics and preserve great quantities in autumn to make tarts. The Laplanders bury them in snow to preserve them through the winter and, at the return of spring, find them as fresh as when first gathered.

Pursue the journey to Bala. Go by the little church of Llangar. Observe somewhat farther on the left,in a field called Caer Bont, a small circular entrenchment consisting of a fosse and rampart with 2 entrances, meant probably as a guard to this pass.

About a mile beyond Llandrillo, I again crossed the Dyfrdwy, at Pont Cilan, a bridge of 2 arches, over a deep and black water. Beyond this spot, the valley acquires near beauties especially on the right. The whole scenery requires the pencil of a Salvator Rosa and here our young artists would find a fit place to study the manner of that great painter of wild nature.

At some distance from Llandderfel bridge, the vale almost closes and finishes nobly at Caletwr with a lofty wooded eminence above which soars the vast mass of the Arenig mountains, notwithstanding they appear immediately after to be very remote. And here I stop a moment to recommended to the traveller who does not choose precisely to follow my steps to follow the course of the Dyfrdwy from Bangor Is-coed through the delicious tract of its waters from thence to Llangollen, Glyndyfrdwy and Corwen, through the matchless vale of Edeirnion to this spot.

On the left lies Rhiwedog (*Bloody Brow*), noted for a battle between Llywarch Hen and the Saxons in which he lost Cynddelw, the last of his numerous sons. A spot not far from hence, called Pabell Llywarch Hen (the tent of that monarch), is supposed to have been the place where he rested the night after the battle and where he finished that pathetic elegy in which he laments the loss of all his sons. In it he directs the last to defend the brow of the hill, indifferent to the fate of the only survivor:

*Cynddelw cadw ditheu y Rhiw*
*Ar a ddêl yma heddiw*
*Cudeb am un mab nyd gwiw.*

Cynddelw, defend thou the brow of yonder hill.
Let the event of the day be what it will:
When there is but one son left,
It is vain to be over-fond of him.

Reach Bala, a small town in the parish of Llanycil noted for its vast trade in woollen stockings and its great markets every Saturday morning when from 200 to 500 pounds worth are sold. Round the place, women and children are in full employ, knitting along the roads; and mixed with them Herculean figures appear, assisting their omphales in this effeminate employ. During winter the females, through love of society, often assemble at one another's houses to knit, sit round a fire and listen to some old tale, some ancient song, or the sound of a harp. This is called Cymorth Gwau or the knitting assembly. Much of the wool is bought at the great fairs at Llanrwst in Dinbych.

Close to the south-east end of the town is a great artificial mount called Tomen y Bala, in the summer time usually covered in a picturesque manner with knitters of both sexes and all ages. This mount appears to have been Roman and placed here with a castelet on its summit to secure the pass towards the sea and keep our mountaineers in subjection. From the summit is a fine view of Llyn Tegid and the adjacent mountains. On the right appear the 2 Arenigs, Fawr and Fach; beyond the farther end soar the lofty Arans with their 2 heads Aran Mawddwy and Penllyn; and beyond all the great Cader Idris closes the view.

The town is of a very regular form and the principal street very spacious; the lesser fall into it at right angles. I will not deny that its origin might have been Roman. Bala takes its name from its vicinity to the place where a river discharges itself from a lake. Balloch in the Erse language signifies the same. The fish are pike, perch, trout, a few roach and abundance of eels, and shoals of that Alpine fish, the Gwyniaid, which spawns in December and are taken in great numbers in spring or summer. Pike have been caught here of 25 pounds weight, a trout of 22, a perch of 10 and a gwyniaid of 5. Sir Watkin Williams Wynn claims the whole fishery of this noble lake.

I digressed to Cerrigydrudion, a parish a few miles to the north noted for certain Druidical remains which gave name to the place. After a dreary ride, I found myself disappointed; these sacred relics having been profanely carried away and converted into a wall. The largest, from drawings preserved by Camden, was a fine specimen of a Celtic cistfaen or stone chest, 10 feet long and near 2 feet 6 inches broad.

Return to Bala and continue my journey along the south side of the lake, a most beautiful ride. Pass by Llanycil church, dedicated to St Beuno and see on the opposite side Llangywer, dedicated to St Gwawr, mother of the Cambrian bard Llywarch Hen.

Caer Gai, placed on an eminence, is said by Camden to have been built by one Caius, a Roman; the Britons ascribe it to Gai, foster-brother to King Arthur. It was probably Roman for multitudes of coins have been found in different parts of the neighbourhood.

Arrive at the foot of Bwlch y Groes (*Pass of The Cross*), one of the most terrible in northern Wales. The height is gained by going up an exceeding steep and narrow zig-zag path to a dreary heathy flat. Here I suppose the cross stood to excite the thanksgiving of travellers for having so well accomplished their arduous journey. The descent on the other side is much greater, and very tedious, into the long and narrow vale of Mawddwy. The roads from the brows of the mountains, in general, are too steep even for a horse; the men therefore carry up on their backs a light sledge, fill it with a very considerable load of turves and drag it, by means of a rope laced over their breast, to the brink of the slope. They then go before it and draw it down, still preceding and guiding its motions which at times have been so violent as to overturn and draw along with it the master to the hazard of his life and not without bodily hurt.

## Chapter Seven

# Dinas Mawddwy to Llanberis

DINAS MAWDDWY, notwithstanding its dignified name, consists but of one street, straight and broad, with houses ill according to a Dinas or city. It still preserves the insignia of power, the stocks and whipping-post, the veg-fawr or great fetter, the mace and standard measure. It is likewise the capital of an extensive lordship under the rule of my worthy cousin, the late John Mytton. The mayor tries criminals but, as the late worthy magistrate (a very honest smith) told me, they have not ventured to whip for some years past. After the wars of the houses of York and Lancaster, multitudes of felons and outlaws established in these parts, stealing and driving whole herds of cattle from one county to another. The traditions respecting these banditti are still extremely strong. I was told that they were so feared that travellers did not dare to go the common road to Shrewsbury but passed over the summits of the mountains to avoid their haunts. The inhabitants placed scythes in the chimneys of their houses to prevent the felons coming down to surprise them in the night, some of which are still to be seen to this day.

Reach Mallwyd, remarkable for the situation of the altar, in the middle of the church, which Doctor Davies, author of the dictionary, then incumbent, in defiance of the orders of Archbishop Laud, removed again from its imaginary superstitious site at the east end.

Pass by some deserted lead mines which, as yet, have never been worked with success. I may here mention an earth which this place is noted for, a bluish ochre which the shepherds wet and use in marking their sheep. Descend along very bad stony roads to Dolgellau, every entrance to which is barred by a turnpike and every approach mended for a short space by help of the scanty tolls. The town is small, the streets disposed in a most irregular manner, but the situation is in a beautiful vale watered by the Wnion.

*Cader Idris*

Cader Idris rises immediately above the town and is generally the object of the traveller's attention. I skirted the mountain for about 2 miles, left on the right the small lake of Llyn Gwernan, and began the ascent along a narrow steep horse-way into Llanfihangel-y-Pennant, perhaps the highest road in Britain, being a common passage even for loaden horses. The hill slopes upwards to Pen y Gadair but the day proved so wet and misty that I lost the enjoyment of the great view from the summit. I could at intervals perceive a stupendous precipice on one side where the hill recedes inwards, forming a theatre with a lake at the bottom. On the other side I saw Craig Cau, a great rock with a lake beneath, possibly the crater of an ancient volcano. This is so excellently expressed by the admirable pencil of my kinsman, Mr Wilson, that I shall not attempt the description. The ingenious Mr Meredith Hughes of Bala assures me that the Pen y Gadair is 950 yards higher than the green at Dolgellau.

Near the river Cregannan, I saw the remains of Llys Bradwen, the court or palace of Ednowen, chief of one of the 15 tribes of North Wales during the reign of Gruffudd ap Cynan or soon after. The structure of the palace shows a low state of architecture and may be paralleled only by the artless fabric of a cattle-house. Ednyfed ap Aaron, a descendant of this great man, had the honour of entertaining Owain Glyndŵr in one of his sad reverses of fortune and is said to have concealed him from the pursuit of his enemies in a cave to this day called Ogof Owain, in the parish of Llangelynnin.

I must not lead the reader into a belief that every habitation of these early times was equal in magnificence to the palace of Ednowen ap Bradwen. Those of inferior gentry were formed of wattles, like Indian wigwams or Highland hovels, for removal from place to place for sake of new pasture or a greater plenty of game. The furniture was correspondent; there were neither tables nor cloths nor napkins. This is less remarkable since we find that, even so late as the time of Edward II, straw was used in the royal apartment. Giraldus informs us that the utmost hospitality was preserved. Every house was open even to the poorest person. When a stranger entered, his arms were taken from him and laid by; and, after the scriptural custom, water was brought to wash his feet. The fare was simple; the meal did not consist of an elegant variety but of numbers of things put together in a large dish. The bread was thin oat-cakes such as are common in our mountainous parts at this time.

Continue the ride, as before, between high mountains in a narrow glen. The road now passes between verdant and smooth hills, the great sheep-walks of the country; they are round at their tops and covered with flocks which yield the materials for the neighbouring manufactures.

I descended a steep pass through fields and, crossing the river, dined on a great stone beneath the vast rock Craig y Deryn (*Rock of Birds*), so called from the numbers of cormorants, rock pigeons and hawks which breed on it. Here the Tywyn is contracted into a fertile vale which extends about 2 miles further. Near its end is a long and high rock, narrow on the top. Here stood the castle which extended lengthways over the whole surface of the summit. The most complete apartment was 36 feet broad, cut out of the rock on 2 sides for much of it is hollowed. It is said to have been once defended by a Coch o'r (Red) Pennant. This probably was Castell y Bere, belonging to our last Llywelyn.

Return about half a mile and ride several miles along the pretty vale of Tal-y-llyn, very narrow but consisting of fine meadows bounded by lofty verdant mountains, very steeply sloped. A few miles beyond Tal-y-llyn church, the hills almost meet at their bottoms. The sides are broken into a thousand crags, many projecting forward in such a manner as to render their fall tremendous. One of the precipices is called Pen-y-delyn from some resemblance to a harp. Another is styled Llam-y-lladron, (*The Thieves' Leap*), from a tradition that thieves were brought here and thrown down. Such a punishment might have been inflicted by order of an arbitrary lord but we formerly very rarely used capital punishments for any crime. Fines were accepted even in cases of murder, giving rise to private revenge and bringing on a train of endless feuds and bloodshed.

Pass over Bwlch Coch and, after descending a very bad road, again reach Dolgellau from whence I visited Nannau, the ancient seat of the Nannau, now of the Vaughans. It is perhaps the highest situation of any gentleman's house in Britain. Above Nannau is a high rock, the top encircled with a dike of loose stones. This had been a Brythonic post, the station perhaps of some tyrant, it being called Moel Orthrwm or the hill of oppression.

Cross the bridge of Llanelltyd. Below is a fine tract of meadow, wretchedly deformed by the necessity of digging into them for turf, the fuel of the country. The tide flows within a small distance of this place and, on the banks, I saw a small sloop ready to be launched. Near the church of Llanelltyd stand the remains of the abbey of Cymer. This had been an abbey of Cistercians founded by the 2 princes Maredudd and Gruffudd about the year 1198.

About 5 or 6 miles from Dolgellau, at Dolmelynllyn, I turned out of the road, meeting the furious course of the Afon Camlan that falls from rock to rock for a very considerable space. It reaches a lofty precipice from which it precipitates into a black pool shaded by trees. Not far from here, a lofty hill forms the forks of the rivers and exhibits a view like those of the shady wilds of America.

After a short ride, see on a common the noted Sarn (or Llwybr) Helen, the causeway or path of Helen, a road supposed to have been made through part of northern Wales by Helena, daughter of Eudda (or Octavius) and wife to the emperor Maximus. The stones which form this road are now entirely covered with turf but the rising is in most parts very visible. The breadth is eight yards and there are tumuli near the highway as was usual with the Romans.

After reposing a night at Rhiw Goch, I continued a few miles to Castell Prysor, a very singular little fort in a pass between the hills on a natural round rock. Notwithstanding the castelet is destitute of mortar, it is probably Roman as multitudes of coins and urns are found about it. The name explains the cause of the want of lime in the walls, Castell Prysor signifying a castle made in haste.

From hence I took the track towards Ffestiniog past Llyn Rathllyn, a small lake noted for a strange variety of perch with a hunched back and the lower part of the backbone, near the tail, oddly distorted. Not far beyond, within the inclosed country, I found a very fine Roman camp called Tomen y Mur or the mount within the wall. Sarn Helen runs into it at one end and is continued to Rhyd yr Halen in Ffestiniog parish.

I returned out of the parish of Trawsfynydd along the beautiful road of the preceding day till I reached Llanelltyd. The ride to Abermaw is very picturesque, the vale watered by the Maw (known here only by the name of Afon, or The River) which widens as we advanced. The sides are bounded by hills and chequered with woods. I found the little town of Abermo seated near the bottom of some high mountains. The houses, placed on the steep sides one above the other, give the opportunity of seeing down the chimneys of their next subjacent neighbours. This is the port of Meirionnydd but not so much frequented as it ought to be. The inhabitants do not attempt commerce on a large scale but vend their manufactures through factors who run away with much of the advantages which the natives might enjoy.

Within a few years were the remains of an ancient tower in which Henry Earl of Richmond used to conceal himself when he came over to consult with his friends about the proposed revolution.

There are few places which abound more in British antiquities than the environs of Corsygedol. This neighbourhood also abounds with cromlechs of very great size. I measured one, in a tenement called Bryn-y-Foel, which was 16 feet 4 inches long, 7 feet broad and 20 inches thick.

*Pass of Drws Ardudwy*

It lay about 2 feet above the ground, supported by small stones, and was surrounded with a circle of loose stones.

This country is in the hundred of Ardudwy. The entrance into it from Trawsfynydd is called Drws Ardudwy, or the door of Ardudwy, formed by nature through the sterile mountains.

I visited an ordinary house called Maes y Garnedd, birth-place of the regicide colonel Jones whose insolence to the neighbouring gentry is still spoken of, even to this day, with much warmth. Actuated by enthusiasm, he went every length that the congenial Cromwell dictated and was a brave and successful office in a cause which, after a certain period, became the foundation of tyranny.

From some of the adjacent heights of this ride, I had a full view beneath me (it being low water) of the long range of sand and gravel which runs from this coast 22 miles into the sea. It is deservedly called Sarn Badrig (or more properly Badrhwyg, *The Ship-breaking Causeway*) from the number of ships lost upon it. This shoal is dry at the ebb of spring-tides and marked in storms by horrible breakers. Tradition says that all this part of the sea had been a habitable hundred called Cantre'r Gwaelod (*Lowland Hundred*) and that it was overwhelmed by the sea about the year 500 in the time of Gwyddno Goronhir.

I pursued my journey towards Harlech but was tempted by my constant fellow-traveller, the reverend Mr John Llwyd, to make a small deviation to the right to visit a near relation of his in Cwm Bychan. The venerable Evan Lloyd with his ancestors boast of being lords of these rocks at least since the year 1100. He and my fellow traveller, being brothers' children, are 18th in descent from Bleddyn ap Cynfyn so the following is a genuine copy of the form of a British pedigree:

Ifan ap Edward, ap Richard, ap Edward, ap Humphrey, ap Edward, ap Dafydd, ap Robert, ap Hywel, ap Dafydd, ap Meurig Llwyd o Nannau, ap Meirig Fychan, ap Ynyr Fychan, ap Ynyr, ap Meurig, ap Madog, ap Cadwgan, ap Bleddyn, ap Cynfyn Prince of North Wales and Powys.

I was introduced to the worthy representative of this long line, who gave me the most hospitable reception in the style of an ancient Welsh. He welcomed us with ale and potent beer, to wash down the Coch yr Wden, or hung goat, and the cheese compounded of the milk of cow and sheep. He likewise showed us the ancient family cup, made of a bull's scrotum, in which large libations had been made in the days of yore. Here the family have lived for many generations, without bettering or lessening their income, without noisy fame but without any of its embittering attendants. Of this house was the valiant Dai Llwyd who is said to have been addressed in the noted Welsh tune Ffarwel Dai Llwyd

*Harlech Castle*

on occasion of his going with Jasper Tudor and Owain Lawgoch to fight Rhisiart Fradwr (or *Richard the Traitor* by which name the Welsh stigmatised *Richard the Third*).

From Cwm Bychan, took the road to Harlech, a small and very poor town remarkable only for its castle which is seated on a lofty rock facing the Irish sea, above an extensive marsh once occupied by the water. This fortress was anciently called Tŵr Branwen from Branwen, sister to Brân ap Llŷr, King of Britain. It was later named Caer Collwyn from Collwyn ap Tango, Lord of Eifionydd, Ardudwy and part of Llŷn. The present castle was the work of Edward I, completed before the year 1283. It was impregnable on the side next to the sea; on the other it was protected by a prodigious fosse cut with vast expense and trouble in the hard rock.

Near this place was found the celebrated piece of antiquity on which the learned have thought fit to bestow the name of torc. The custom of wearing the torc was continued to later times. Llywelyn, a Lord of Yale, was called Llywelyn aur Dorchog (*Llywelyn with the Golden Torch*) on that account. The common proverb *Mi a dynna'r dorch â chwi* (I will pluck the torc with you) signifies, to this day, a hard struggle of a person before he would yield a victory.

From Harlech I ascended a very steep hill and on my way observed several maen hirion and circles formed of large common pebble-stones, sometimes circle within circle. This place is called Bonllef Hir or the Cry to Battle. Possibly it had been a field of combat and a chieftain fell here for one of the maen hirion is of distinguished size.

From hence the road is tolerably bad and stony till I reach Glyn, a house of my kinsman Robert Godolphin Owen, seated in a well wooded romantic bottom. This had been the residence of the ancient family of the Wynnes from whom it passed to the Owens by the marriage of Sir Robert with the heiress of the place in the last century.

Pass by the village of Llandecwyn. The narrow path we rode on impends over Llyn Tecwyn and is cut out of a hill whose sides are composed of shivering slate starting out at an immense height above, threatening destruction. They were much enlivened by flocks of milk-white goats which skipped along the points and looked down on us with much unconcern. From one of the heights, the stupendous mountains of Gwynedd and those of Meirionnydd, not much inferior, form a tremendous scenery. The highest summit of Eryri, called Yr Wyddfa, soars pre-eminent. From thence the mountains gradually lower to Llŷn which stretches in view far to the west and terminates on the point of Aberdaron.

After a short ride, reach the village and chapel of Maentwrog, dependent on the church of Ffestiniog. Near one end is a great upright stone called Maen Twrog from a saint of that name who built the church of Llandwrog.

At Tan y Bwlch is a very neat small inn for the reception of travellers, who ought to think themselves much indebted to the present Earl of Radnor for the great improvement it received from his munificence. Above it is a house embosomed with woods, most charmingly situated on the side of the hill. This seat, from the quick succession of owners by the fatal attachment to the bottle, has occasioned many a moral reflection from the English traveller.

The river hereabouts widens into a good salmon fishery and, after some space, falls into an arm of the sea called Traeth Bach or the little sands.

Ride up the vale and, dismounting, meet the course of the Cynfael which tumbles along the bottom of a deep and time-worn chasm. About a mile from the Cynfael is another comfortable inn which has often received me after my toilsome expeditions. Opposite to it lies Cwmorthin, a retreat much more sequestered and much more difficult of access than even Cwm-bychan.

Not 2 miles from Ffestiniog, on the road from Trawsfynydd to Ysbyty, I fell again into Ffordd Helen which is here quite bare and exhibits the rude stones from which it was made. Near it, at Rhyd yr Halen, on the right, are the remains of Beddau Gwŷr Ardudwy, or the graves of the men of Ardudwy. These graves were about 6 feet long, marked at each end by 2 upright stones but most of the stones are now removed. There are yet to be seen several circles of stones, the largest about 52 feet in diameter. The tradition relating to these monuments is classical, nearly parallel with the rape of the Sabines. The men of Ardudwy, to populate their country, made an inroad into the vale of Clwyd and laid violent hands on the fair ladies of the land; they carried them in safety to this place where they were overtaken by the warriors of the vale. A fierce battle ensued and the men of Ardudwy were slain. But the ravishers had so gained the hearts of their fair prey that, on their defeat, the ladies, rather than return home, rushed into an adjacent water and there perished.

From hence I descended the long and tedious steep of Bwlch Carreg y Frân into the narrow vale of Penmachno, turning right to visit Llyn Conwy. It is placed the highest of any piece of water I have met with in these parts. In it are 3 islands, one of which is the haunt of the black-back gulls during the breeding season. They are so fierce in the defence of their young that I know of a man who was nearly drowned in an attempt to swim to their nests. He was so violently beaten by the old birds that he though he escaped well with the dreadful bruises he received on all the upper part of his body. The water issues out of the end of the lake in the form of a little rill but, in the course of a few miles before it reaches Llanrwst, becomes the considerable river Conwy by the addition of the various mountain streams.

Descend for 2 or 3 miles and reach the village of Ysbyty Ifan or the hospital of St John of Jerusalem, so styled from its having formed, in the then inhospitable country, an asylum and guard for travellers under the protection of the knights who held the manor and made its precincts a sanctuary. After the abolition of the order, this privilege became the bane of the neighbourhood; for the place, thus exempted from all jurisdiction, was converted into a den of thieves and murderers who ravaged the country far and wide with impunity till the reign of Henry VII when they were extirpated by the bravery and prudence of Maredudd ap Ifan.

After a very long interval, another charity succeeded as an the alms-houses for 6 poor men, founded in 1600 by captain Richard Vaughan, a poor knight of Windsor descended from the neighbouring house of Pant Glas.

From Ysbyty I made an excursion to Foelas, about 2 miles distant, remarkable for a great column with an inscription in memory of Llywelyn, Prince of Wales, who was slain in the year 1021. Here is likewise a vast artificial mount, the site of a Welsh castelet destroyed by Llywelyn the Great.

Turn back and again reach the river Conwy and, after a short ride, arrive at its celebrated falls, not very far from its junction with the Machno. The prospect is very extraordinary, from the neighbourhood of a fulling mill, where the channel of the rivers forms a triangle of deep and doleful chasms worn by the water through the live rock. Not far below begins the cataract, the most tremendous I ever saw and whose roaring gives sufficient notice of its vicinity.

Descend a steep hill and arrive in Nant Conwy, or the vale of Conwy, after passing over Pont-ar-Ledr beneath which the Afon Lledr hastens to join that which gives name to the valley. Observe, in the course of the Conwy, a deep, wide and still water called Llyn yr Afanc (Beavers' Pool) from being, in old times, the haunt of those animals. Their skin was in such esteem as to be valued at 120 pence while that of the martin took no more than 24 pence, and an ermine, otter, wolf or fox only 12 pence. They seem to have been the chief finery and luxury of the days of Hywel Dda.

The vale gradually expands from this end and extends about 20 miles,

*Falls of the Conwy*

terminating at the town of Conwy. It soon widens to about a mile in breadth and improves in beauty, especially in the neighbourhood of Llanrwst where it is divided into the most beautiful meadows. The sides of the hills are finely cultivated; on the western, the vast mountains of Eryri rise in a majestic range; the eastern consists of low and broken hills, chequered with rich pasturage, cornfields and groves. The river meanders through the whole and, before it reaches Llanrwst, is of a considerable size.

Visit the church of Betws Wyrion Iddon, or the bede-house of the grandchildren of Iddon. Within is the figure of Gruffudd ap Dafydd Goch, son to Dafydd Goch, natural son of Dafydd, brother to the last Prince of Wales.

A little farther, pass by Pont-y-pair, a most singular bridge flung over the Llugwy, consisting of 5 arches placed on the rude rocks which form most durable piers. These rocks are precipitous and, in high floods, exhibit to the passenger most awful cataracts below the bridge. The scenery beyond, of rocky mountains, fringed with woods, is very striking.

I soon left the bridge and, after a steep ascent, arrive at Dolwyddelan castle, seated in a rocky valley sprinkled over with stunted trees and watered by the Lledr. The boundaries are rude and barren mountains, among others the great bending mountain Siabod which is often conspicuous from distant places.

The castle is placed on a high rock, precipitous on one side, and insulated. It consists of 2 square towers, one 40 feet by 25, the other 31 by 20. Each had formerly 3 floors. The materials of the fortress are the shattery stone of the country, yet well squared, the masonry good and the mortar hard. The castle-yard lay between the towers.

This had been founded by some of our princes but we are ignorant of its origin. There were very few castles in northern Wales before its conquest by the English. They were needless for nature created, in our rocks and mountains, fortifications (until our fatal divisions) quite impregnable. Had there been occasion for artificial retreats, the wealth of our country could readily have supplied the means of erecting them. We had the balance of trade in our favour. This prevented our princes from ever making use of their third prerogative, that of coining. Our herds and flocks were the frequent resource of the English and brought large sums into Wales. Witness the large sums of money we too frequently were obliged to pay as purchases of a disgraceful peace. Besides, cash was far from being requisite since every subject except the king's husbandmen was bound by our laws to assist in building the royal castles.

Iorwerth Drwndwn made this place his residence and here is said to have been born his son, Llywelyn the Great, who began his reign in the time of Richard I. Hywel ap Ifan ap Rhys Gethin, a noted outlaw, later resided here. This gentleman soon reformed the country, establishing colonies of the "most tall and able men" he could procure till at least these amounted to 140 tall bowmen, every one arrayed in a "jacket or armolet coate, a good steele cap, a short sword and dagger, together with his bows and arrows; many of them also had horses and chasing slaves which were ready to answer the cry on all occasions". We are indebted to 'Gwedir Family', a publication by my respected friend the honourable Daines Barrington.

In my return to Pont-y-pair, digressed a little up the river Llugwy to see a noted cascade called Rhaeadr Ewynnol (Waterfall of Foam, wrongly translated as Swallow Falls). The river runs along a straight stony channel for a considerable way, amidst narrow meadows bounded by majestic Alpine scenery, then falls into an amazing hollow. The bottom is difficult of access but, when arrived at, exhibits a wonderful scene of mountain and precipice shaded with trees which fringe the top and start even from the fissures of the sides.

Cross Pont-y-pair and go beneath a very lofty rock clothed with wood, called Carreg Gwalch (*Falcon Rock*). Here was the retreat of a famous partisan of the house of Lancaster, who lurked in a cave still named from him Ogo Dafydd ap Shenkin.

The ancient house of Gwydir stands near the foot of this rock. It is built round a greater and lesser court. Over the gate-way is the date 1558 with I.W. (John Wynne ap Maredudd, grandfather to the famous Sir John, author of the memoirs of the family). This shows 1553, the supposed death of the former, to be a mistake. The place takes its name from Gawed dir, the bloody land, from the battles fought here by Llywarch Hen about the year 610, or perhaps from the cruel battle in 952 between the sons of Hywel and the princes Ieuan and Iago; a third may be added, between Gruffudd ap Cynan and Trahaearn ap Caradog, equally bloody. The supposition that it was derived from its being the first house in Wales which had glass windows is not well founded, those conveniences having been known long before.

Among various papers belonging to Gwydir is a curious one drawn up by old Sir John Wynne, prescribing the rules to his chaplain, an odd mixture of insolence and piety. The inventory of his wardrobe, drawn up in his own hand, shows not only the complete dress of a man of rank in those days but the great economy of the times, among people of fashion, when their wardrobe was bestowed by will and passed from generation to generation.

From hence to Llanrwst is a pretty walk, mostly by the side of the river. The town lies in Dinbych on the opposite bank. The approach is over the bridge, the boasted plan of Inigo Jones. I wish I could do more honour to my country than suppose him to have been a descendant of this neighbourhood but he seems to have been a by birth a Londoner (son of a cloth worker who in all probability was a native of Wales); his real christian name was Ynyr which he changed into Inigo or Ignatius.

I made from Llanrwst 2 excursions, one to visit Maenan Abbey, translated hither in 1289 from Conwy by permission of pope Nicholas at the request of Edward I. A large old house, built from the materials of the abby, still remains.

Returned through Llanrwst, about 2 miles beyond, high over the Conwy. Visit the village of Trefriw where numbers of small vessels are built and sent down the river at spring tides. It is said that Llywelyn the Great had a palace near this place and, as a proof, several hewn stones have been found in ploughing a field called Gardd y Neuadd. The church of Trefriw was originally built by Llywelyn for the ease of his princess who before was obliged to foot it to Llanrhychwyn, a long walk among the mountains.

From hence I went back as far as Gwydir and ascended a very steep hill, leaving the park belonging to the house on the left. The Sorbus Aucuparia or mountain ash is frequent in these parts. The poorer sort of people make a drink called diodgriafel by infusing the berries in water. In former times, a superstitious use was made of the wood: a piece made in the form of a cross was carried in the pocket as an infallible preservative against all sorts of fascinations.

After gaining the summit, visit to the right Llyn Geirionydd, a small lake noted for having had near it the habitation of the celebrated Taliesin who flourished about the year 560 in the time of Gwyddno Goronhir, a petty prince of Cantre'r Gwaelod. The history of our famous bard begins like that of Moses for he was found exposed on the water, wrapped in a leathern bag. Elfin, son of Gwyddno, took pity on the infant and caused proper care to be taken of him.

From this lake I descended a great steep into Glyn Llugwy, a bottom watered by the Llugwy, fertile in grass and varied by small groves of young oaks very unlike the great woods which clothed this place, Dyffryn Mymbyr, Llanberis and other parts of Eryri in the time of Leland. The small church of Capel Curig and a few scattered houses give life to this dreary tract. Yr Wyddfa and all his sons, Crib Goch, Crib y Ddysgl, Lliwedd, Yr Aran and many others here burst at once into full view and make this the finest approach to our boasted Alps.

Tryfan & Llyn Ogwen

The boundaries of this vale are, on one side, the base of the crooked mountain Moel Siabod; on the other that of Glyder Fach and several other hills of note. The bottom is meadowy, at this time enlivened with the busy work of hay harvest and filled with drags, horses and even men and women, loaden with hay. The middle is varied with 2 small lakes along whose sides we rode. At some distance beyond them, near Penygwryd, we quitted our horses to visit the summit of the Glyder noted for the singular disposition of the rocks. We directed our servants to go on to Llanberis with our steeds.

The ascent was extremely long, steep and laborious, wet and slippery, and almost the whole way covered with loose fragments of rocks beneath which was a continual roar of waters seeking their way to the bottom.

Our pains were fully repaid on attaining the summit. The area was covered with groups of columnar stones of vast size, from 10 to 30 feet long, lying in all directions. The tops are frequently crowned in the strangest manner with other stones lying on them horizontally. One was about 25 feet long and 6 broad. I climbed up and, stamping with my foot, felt a strong tremulous motion from end to end. Another, 11 feet long and 6 in circumference in the thinnest part, was poised so nicely on the point of a rock that, to appearance, the touch of a child would overset it. A third enormous mass had the property of a rocking stone. Many of the stones had shells bedded in them, and in their neighbourhood I found several pieces of lava.

One side of this mountain is formed into a gap with sharp rocks pointing upwards, one above the other, to a great height. In the midst of a vale far below rises the singular mountain Tryfan, assuming on this side a pyramidal form, naked and very rugged.

From Glyder Fach I passed over a plain above half a mile broad, called Y Waun Oer (*The Chilly Mountainous Flat*). Observe from the edge, in a tremendous hollow, Llyn Bochllwyd (*Lake of the Grey Goat*), and in the bottom of the valley near the foot of the Tryfan, Llyn Ogwen, noted for its fine trout.

From Y Waen Oer we made a most hazardous descent to Cwm Bochlwyd and from thence to Llyn Ogwen. The way from that place into the valley, or rather chasm, of Nant Ffrancon is called Benglog, the most dreadful horse path in Wales, worked in the rudest manner into steps for a great length. On one side, in a deep hollow formed under fallen rocks, was once the hiding place of Rhys Goch o'r Eryri, (*Rhys the Red of Eryri*). Rhys was a mountain bard patronised by Robert ap Maredudd, a partisan of Owain Glyndŵr of whose fortunes he partook. From the bottom of Nant Ffrancon, I have seen the shepherds skipping from peak to peak but the point of contact was so small that they seemed to my uplifted eyes like beings of another order floating in the air.

The Tryfan from this bottom makes also a very singular appearance, resembling a human face reclined backward. Forehead, nose, lips and chin are very apparent and you may add without any strain of fancy the beard of an ancient inhabitant, an arch-druid.

Begin another hard ascent to Cwm Idwal, infamous for the murder of the young prince Idwal (son of Owain Gwynedd) by Dunawd, son of Nefydd Hardd, to whom Owain had entrusted the youth to be fostered according to the custom of the country. It was a fit place to inspire murderous thoughts, environed with horrible precipices shading a lake lodged at its bottom. The shepherds fable that it is the haunt of demons and that no bird dare fly over its damned water. Near this place is a quarry, noted for excellent hones, of which quantities are sent annually to London.

Observe on the right a stupendous split rock called Twll Du (*The Devil's Kitchen*). It is a horrible gap in the centre of a great black precipice extending in length about 150 yards, in depth about 100, and only 6 wide, perpendicularly open to the surface of the mountain. On surmounting my difficulties, and taking a little breath, I ventured to look down this dreadful aperture and found its horrors far from being lessened in my exalted situation, for to it were added the waters of Llyn y Cŵn impetuously rushing through its bottom.

Glyder Fawr is connected to the lesser Glyder by the Waun Oer. The traveller therefore has his choice of ways to these wondrous mountains but the most preferable for ease is the road I descend into the vale of Llanberis. In my way, pass close by a rugged brow of a hill which I think is Rhiw y Glyder, recorded by Llwyd and Ray for its variety of plants. Soon after, visit the small lake called Llyn y Cŵn. Giraldus informs us that in his days the 3 kinds of fish it yielded (trouts, perch and eels) were monocular, every one wanting the left eye. At present there is not a fish in it to disprove the relation though many rare plants are to be met with.

Leave on the right Elidir Fawr and Elidir Fach, 2 great mountains, part of the boundaries of Nant Peris, and arrive in that vale by Esgair y Ceunant. This is a very picturesque vale, bounded by the base of Yr Wyddfa, Cefn Cwm Gafr, the Glyderau and the two Elidir, each of them first-rate mountains. It is straight and of nearly an equal breadth, filled by some meadows and 2 magnificent lakes which communicate to each other by means of a river. The venerable oaks spoken of by Leland are no more. Avarice or dissipation (and its constant follower, poverty) have despoiled much of our principality of its leafy beauties. A succession of rude and stony stairs made with much labour once ran on one side high above the lake and was often cut out of the rock to form the way. This is, I am now informed, changed into a road, which too much facilitates the approach and lessens its propriety and its agreement with the wild environs.

# Chapter Eight

# Llanberis to Beddgelert

**ON THE** loftiest part, over one of the lakes, stand the remains of Castell Dolbadarn, consisting of a round tower and a few fragments of walls. It was constructed with the thin laminated stones of the country, cemented with very strong mortar without shells. The inner diameter of the tower is only 26 feet. This seems to have been built to defend the pass into the interior parts of Eryri and was likewise used as a state prison. The founder was evidently a Welsh prince. I am informed that it was Padarn Beisrudd, son of Idwal.

In this valley are two groups of wretched houses. The farthest is near the end of the upper lake, with its church dedicated to St Peris who was, we are told, a cardinal. Here is to be seen the well of the saint, inclosed with a wall. The sibyl of the place attends and divines your fortune by the appearance or non-appearance of a little fish which lurks in some of its holes.

From hence I took a ride above the lakes to their lower extremity. The upper is the lesser but much the most beautiful piece of water. It is said to be in places 140 yards deep and to have abounded with char before they were reduced by the streams flowing from the copper mines which had been worked on the sides of the hills.

The lower lake is about a mile and a half long, narrows gradually into the form of a river called the Rhythallt, and flows in a diffused channel to Caernarfon where it assumes the name of Seiont. Near this end of the lake lived a celebrated personage whom I was disappointed in not finding at home. This was Margaret uch Ifan of Penllyn, the last specimen of the strength and spirit of the ancient British fair. She is at this time (1786) about 90 years of age. This extraordinary female was the greatest hunter, shooter and fisher of her time. She kept a dozen at least of dogs, terriers, greyhounds and spaniels, all excellent in their kinds. She killed more foxes in one year than all the confederate hunts do in ten, rowed stoutly and was queen of the lake, fiddled excellently and knew all our old music, did not neglect the mechanic arts for she was a very good joiner, and at the age of 70 was the best wrestler in the country; few young men dared to try a fall with her.

Some years ago she had a maid of congenial qualities but death, that mighty hunter, at last earthed this faithful companion. Margaret was also a blacksmith, shoemaker, boat-builder and maker of harps. She shoed her own horses, made her own shoes and was under contract to convey the copper ore down the lakes. All the neighbouring bards payed their addresses to Margaret and celebrated her exploits in pure British verse. At length, she gave her hand to the most effeminate of her admirers as if predetermined to maintain the superiority which nature had bestowed on her.

About half a mile farther, I visited the remains of Llys Dinorwig, a house said to have been one of the palaces of prince Llywelyn ap Gruffudd: the walls high and strong, the hall 24 yards long, and before the house is a deep ditch over which had probably been a drawbridge. Not very far from hence is a spot called Rhiw'r Cyrn (*Brow of the Horns*) where, according to the old usage, an officer stood and blew his horn to give notice to the household of the approach of their master or to summon the vassals to assemble on all emergent occasions.

This country is part of the woodless flat between the mountains and the Menai. Its want of strength is supplied with several posts fortified in the Celtic manner. Dinas Dinorwig, half a mile south-east of the church of Llanddeiniolen, is the chief. The area is very large, surrounded with an agger of small stones backed by another of very large ones; then succeeds a deep ditch, a rampart of earth, a second vast ditch, and a third rampart. Within the area is a circle of stones, the post probably of the commander in chief. To the east is a strong chalybeate water, formerly in much repute. It is called Ffynnon Cegin Arthur (*Water of King Arthur's Kitchen*) and is the source of Afon Cegin which falls into the sea between Bangor and Penrhyn.

In our way from hence, we passed by another, called Pen y Gaer, and soon after by a smaller called Bryn y Costrelau surrounded by a single wall. On a rising on the other side of the Rhythallt is another, named Caer Cwm y Glo, or Caer Carreg-y-Frân, from which had been (as we were informed) a paved way to Llys Dinorwig. I may here add that, after the death of Llywelyn, Edward I bestowed that palace on Sir Gruffudd Llwyd, the same gentleman who first brought him the news of the birth

*Snowdon from Cwm y Glo*

of his son Edward of Caernarfon.

Return by the same road and, after refreshing myself with a night's rest at Mr Close's (agent to the mines in Llanberis), early in the morning begin our ascent to the highest peak of Eryri under the guidance of Hugh Shone whom I beg leave to recommend as a most able conductor. Keep upon the side of the lake for a considerable way then turn to the left and see Ceunant Mawr, not far from the road, a noble cataract precipitating over 2 vast rocks into 2 most horrible chasms. Near this place were found several beads; some of glass, and one of jet. The beads and a remarkable shell found in the same place are in the possession of the Reverend John Llwyd of Caerwys. The beads are known in Gwynedd by the name of Glain Neidr and are worn as amulets against the chin-cough et cetera.

Ascend above Cwm Brwynog, a very deep bottom fertile in Gwair y Rhosydd which is composed chiefly of different kinds of rushes, particularly Juncus Squarosus (the moss-rush), Scirpus Caespitosus (the heath club rush), Schaenus Nigricans (the black bog rush) and Carexes intermixed with a few kinds of grass. The hay which the lower meadows produce is very different in quality, being remarkably fine and soft, and consists in great part of the fine bent grass Agrostis Capillaris.

This mountainous tract scarcely yields any corn. Its produce is cattle and sheep, which, during summer, keep very high in the mountains, followed by their owners with their families who reside in that season in hafodtai or summer dairy-houses as the farmers in the Swiss alps do in their Sennes. These houses consist of a long low room with a hole at one end to let out the smoke from the fire which is made beneath. Their furniture is very simple: stones are the substitutes of stools and the beds are of hay, ranged along the sides. They manufacture their own clothes and dye their cloth with Cenn du y Cerrig, or *Lichen omphaloides*; and another Cenn, the *Lichen parietinus* (native dyes collected from the rocks). During summer, the men pass their time either in harvest work or in tending their herds; the women in milking, or making butter and cheese. For their own use, they milk both ewes and goats, and make cheese of the milk, for their own consumption. The diet of these mountaineers is very plain, consisting of butter, cheese, and oat-bread, or bara ceirch; they drink whey but have a reserve of a few bottles of very strong beer, by way of cordial, in illness. They are people of good understanding, wary and circumspect, usually tall, thin, and of strong constitutions, from their way of living. Towards winter, they descend to their hen dref, or old dwelling, where they lead, during that season, a vacant life.

Snowdon from Capel Curig

In the course of our ascent, saw on the left, above the Cwm, Moel Cynghorion *(Hill of Council)*. Pass through Bwlch Maes-cwm and skirt the side of Yr Wyddfa till we reach Bwlch Cwm Brwynog where the ascent becomes very difficult on account of its vast steepness. People here usually quit their horses. We began a toilsome march, clambering among the rocks. On the left were the precipices over Cwm Brwynog with Llyn Du'r Arddu at their foot. On our right were those over the small lakes Llyn Glas, Llyn-y-Nadroedd, and Llyn Coch. The last is the highest on this side of the mountain; and, on whose margins, we were told, that, in fairy days, those diminutive gentry kept their revels. This space between precipice and precipice formed a short and not very agreeable isthmus, till we reached a verdant expanse which gave us some respite, before we laboured up another series of broken crags: after these is a second smooth tract reaching almost to the summit which, by way of pre-eminence, is styled Yr Wyddfa *(The Conspicuous)*. It rises almost to a point, or, at best, there is but room for a circular wall of loose stones, within which travellers usually take their repast.

The mountain from hence seems propped by 4 vast buttresses; between which are 4 deep cwms or hollows; each, excepting one, has one or more lakes, lodged in its distant bottom. The nearest was Ffynnon Las, Green Well, lying immediately below us. One of the company had the curiosity to descend a very bad way to a jutting rock that impeded over the monstrous precipice. He seemed like Mercury ready to take his flight from the summit of Atlas. The waters of Ffynnon Las from this height appeared black and unfathomable, and the edges quite green. From thence is a succession of bottoms surrounded by lofty and rugged hills, the greatest part of whose sides are perfectly mural and form the most magnificent amphitheatre in nature. Yr Wyddfa is on one side; Crib y Ddysgl, with its serrated tops, on another; Crib Goch, a ridge of fiery redness, appears beneath the preceding; and opposite to it is the boundary called the Lliwedd. Another very singular support to this mountain is Y Clawdd Coch, rising into a sharp ridge, so narrow as not to afford breadth even for a path.

The view from this exalted situation is unbounded. I have seen Eryri from the county of Chester, the high hills of Yorkshire, part of the north of England, Scotland and Ireland. A plain view of the Isle of Man and that of Ynys Môn lay extended like a map beneath me, with every rill visible. I took much pains to see this prospect to advantage: sat up at a farm on the west till about 12, and walked up the whole way. The night was remarkably fine and starry. Towards morn, the stars faded away and left a short interval of darkness which was soon dispersed by the dawn of the day. The body of the sun appeared most distinct, with the rotundity of the moon, before it rose high enough to render its beam too brilliant for our sight; the sea which bounded the western part was gilt by its rays, first in slender streaks, at length glowing with redness. The prospect was disclosed like the gradual drawing up of a curtain in a theatre. We saw more and more till the heat became so powerful as to attract the mists from the various lakes, which in a slight degree obscured the prospect. The shadow of the mountain was flung many miles and showed its bicapitated form; Yr Wyddfa making one head, Crib y Ddysgl the other. I counted this time between 20 and 30 lakes, either in this county or Meirionnydd. The day proved so excessively hot that my journey cost me the skin of the lower part of my face before I reached the resting-place after the fatigue of the morning.

On this day (August 15th), the sky was obscured very soon after I got up. A vast mist enveloped the whole circuit of the mountain. The prospect down was horrible. It gave an idea of numbers of abysses concealed by thick smoke furiously circulating around us. Very often a gust of wind formed an opening in the clouds which gave a fine and distinct vista of lake and valley. Sometimes they opened only in one place; at others, in many at once, exhibiting a most strange and perplexing sight of water, fields, rocks or chasms, in 50 different places. They then closed at once and left us involved in darkness. In a small space they would separate again and fly in wild eddies round the middle of the mountains and exposing, in parts, both tops and bases clear to our view. We descended from this various scene with great reluctance but a thunder-storm overtook us before we reached our horses. Its rolling among the mountains was inexpressibly awful and the rain uncommonly heavy. We remounted our horses and gained the bottom with great hazard. The little rills which had trickled along the sides of the mountain during our ascent were now swelled into torrents. We and our steeds passed with utmost risk of being swept away by these sudden waters. At length we arrived safe, yet sufficiently wet and dreary, at our former quarters.

It is very rare that the traveller gets a proper day to ascend the hill. It often appears clear but, by the evident attraction of the clouds, this lofty mountain becomes suddenly and unexpectedly enveloped in mist. At times I have observed the clouds lower to half their height and, notwithstanding they had been dispersed to the right and left, yet they have met from both sides and united to involve the summit in one great obscurity.

The quantity of water which flows from the lakes of Eryri is very considerable, so much that I doubt not but collectively they would exceed the waters of the Thames before it meets the flux of the ocean.

The reports of the height of this noted hill have been very differently given. A Mr Caswell, who was employed by Mr Adams, in 1682, measured it by instruments made by the directions of Mr Flamstead and asserts its height to be 1,240 yards: but for the honour of our mountain I am sorry to say that I must give greater credit to the experiments made of late years, which have sunk it to 1,189 yards and one foot, reckoning from the quay at Caernarfon to the highest peak.

The stone that composes this, and indeed the greatest part of Eryri, is excessively hard. Large coarse crystals are often found in the fissures, and very frequently cubic pyrites: the usual attendants on Alpine tracts. These are also frequented by the rock-ouzel, a mountain bird, and some of the lakes are stocked with char and Gwyniad, Alpine fish. The ancient inhabitant, the goat, decreases daily in value since the decline of orthodoxal wigs to which its snowy hair universally contributed. Large flocks are still kept for the dairy and milked with great regularity.

The animals of these regions are chiefly foxes. Stags were found here in the days of Leland in such numbers as to destroy the little corn which the farmers attempted to sow but they were extirpated before the year 1626. Eryri being a royal forest, warrants were issued for the killing of the deer.

Yr Wyddfa was held as sacred by the ancient Brython as Parnassus was by the Greeks and Ida by the Cretans. It is still said that whoever slept on Yr Wyddfa would wake up inspired as much as if he had taken a nap on the hill of Apollo. The Welsh had always the strongest attachment to the tract of Eryri. Edward I was told by the inhabitants of Eryri, in the treaty he held with our countrymen in the year 1281, that even should their prince by inclined to gratify the king in yielding him possession, they would not do homage to strangers of whose tongue, manners and laws they were ignorant. Our princes had, in addition to their title, that of Lord of Snowdon. Such was the importance of this strong region that Llywelyn, when at the last extremity, rejected Edward's proposal of 1,000 years and some honourable county in England, well knowing his principality must terminate with the cession.

No sooner had Edward effected his conquest than he held a triumphal fair upon this our chief of mountains and adjourned to finish the joy of his victory by solemn tournaments on the plains of Nefyn.

I shall take my leave of Eryri with some remarks on the name and weather. The first is a literal translation of the ancient appellation Creigie'r Eira, (*The Snowy Mountains*), from the frequency of snow upon

*Nant Peris with the Glyder & Crib Goch*

them. The earliest appearance of snow is commonly between the middle of October and the beginning of November: the falls which happen then are usually washed away with the rains and the hills remain clear till Christmas. Between that time and the end of January, the greatest falls happen. These are succeeded by others about the latter end of April or the beginning of May, which remain in certain places till the middle of June. It has even happened that the greatest fall has been in April or the beginning of May, and that never fails happening when the preceding winter has had the smallest falls. But the fable of Giraldus concerning the continuance of snow the whole year is totally to be exploded.

Near the end of Nant Peris, pass beneath Glyder Fawr and observe the strata of a columnar form, high above our heads. At times, vast fragments of this tremendous rock tumble down; the ruins are scattered about the base and exhibit awful specimens of the frequent lapses. One is styled the Cromlech for having accidentally fallen on other stones; it remains lifted from the earth with a hollow beneath, resembling one of those Druidical antiquities. The length of the incumbent stone is 60 feet, the breadth 46, the thickness 16. The hollow is said once to have been occupied by an old woman but now serves as a sheep pen.

The ascent from here is either over loose stones or solid staircase and is exceedingly steep. It is a singular road lying in a stupendous chasm bounded for above a mile by nearly equidistant precipices of prodigious height; on one side belonging to the Glyderau and on the other by parts of Snowdon.

Refresh ourselves on a spot called Gorphwysfa (*The Resting Place*). At a small distance is Bwlch y Gwyddel (*Pass of the Irishmen*) from whence is a singular view of Dyffryn Mymbyr, the chasm we had left, and far below us the picturesque vale of Nant Gwynant, the scene of many a bloody skirmish in the time of Edward IV between William Earl of Pembroke and the Welsh Lancastrians under Ieuan ap Robert.

Descend a very steep road, into that part called Cwm Dyli; where we quitted our horses, and began a most toilsome journey to visit the hidden vales lodged in the bosom of the mountains. We began with clambering up the rugged face of a rock, broken into a multitude of short precipices, and divided in the middle by a cataract, the discharge of the waters from the Alpine lakes. After about a quarter of a mile's labour, we reach Cwm Dyli, a flat tract of hay ground watered by a river and filled with hay makers, the farmer and his family being resident here in his hafodtai for the summer season. After dining with them on curds and whey, we kept along the river's side and found opposed to us another front, rugged as the former and attended with a cataract. This was surmounted with

*Llyn Gwynan*

equal difficulty. We found, on arriving at the top, an hollow a mile in length filled with Llyn Llydaw, a fine lake, winding beneath the rocks and vastly indented by rocky projections here and there jutting into it. In it was one little island, the haunt of black-backed Gulls which breed here and, alarmed by such unexpected visitants, broke the silence of this sequestered place by their deep screams.

We continued our walk, ascending along a narrow path above the lake as far as the extremity; then descending, reached the opposite side in order to encounter a third descent as arduous as the preceding. This brought us into the horrible crater, immediately beneath the great precipice of Yr Wyddfa, in which is lodged Ffynnon Las. Its situation is the most dreadful, surrounded by more than 3 parts of a circle, with the most horrible precipices of Yr Wyddfa, Crib y Ddysgl and Crib Goch, with the vast mural steeps of Lliwedd, continued over the other lake and Cwm Dyli. In the Lliwedd was a strange break called Bwlch y Saethau (*Pass of the Arrows*), probably a station for hunters to watch the wanderings of the deer.

The margins of Ffynnon Las here appeared to be shallow and gravelly. The waters had a greenish cast but the rocks reflected into them seemed varied with stripes of the richest colours, like the most beautiful lute strings, and changed almost to infinity. Here we observed the Wheat-ear, a small and seemingly tender bird, and which is almost the only small one, or indeed the only one, except the rock ouzel or mwyalchen y graig, that frequents these heights; the reason is evidently the want of food.

We descended from this dreary scene, on the other side of the hill, above Llyn Llydaw, having the tremendous red precipices of Crib Goch high above us, rising into a mere ridge, serrated its whole length. The faces of many of the rocks were marked with large veins of coarse white crystal; and others, especially Crib Goch, were varied with the deep green of the dwarf Alpine Juniper. On attaining the tops of the hills above the lower end of the lake, we descended to the Gorphwysfa where we found our horses and returned once more into Nant Gwynant. This is the most beautiful vale in Eryri, varied with woods, lakes, river and meadows, and guarded on each side by vast mountains such as Crib Du, or part of Nantmor, the Aran, Lliwedd, Dduallt and Wenallt, extending about 5 miles to the church of Beddgelert.

Near the end of the lake, the valley grows so contracted as to form only a narrow straight but almost instantly opens again into a fine expanse chiefly filled with the beautiful Llyn Dinas. Beyond that is a tract of meads, chequered with woods and watered by the river created by the various lakes but retaining the name of Afon Glaslyn from the lofty

*Llyn Dinas & Moel Hedog*

lake whence it originates.

At the bottom rises a vast rock, insulated and clothed with wood: the famous Dinas Emrys from early times celebrated in British story. When Gwrtheyrn (Vortigern) found himself unable to contest with the treacherous Saxons whom he had invited to Britain in the year 449, he determined, by the advice of his magicians, on building an impregnable fortress in Snowdon. He collected the materials, which all disappeared in one night. The prince, astonished at this, convened again his wise men. They assured him his building would never stand unless it was sprinkled with the blood of a child born without the help of a father. The realm was ransacked. At length one of his emissaries overheard some boys at play reproach another and call him an unbegotten knave. The child and his mother were brought before the king. She confessed he was the offspring of an Incubus, a species of being now unhappily out of all credit. The boy, whose name was Merlin, was ordered to be sacrificed but confounded all the magicians with his questions and, explaining the cause of the miscarriage, got his liberty.

Merlin, or Myrddin Emrys, or Ambrosius, was in fact the son of a noble Roman of the same name. His mother, a Vestal, to save her life and honour, invented the fable of his father, which was swallowed by the credulity of the times. Merlin became an able mathematician and astronomer, deeply read in all the learning of his age. The vulgar, as usual, ascribed all he did to art magic and his discovery that Vortigern had begun to found his castle on a morass was immediately said to have been attended with most portentous circumstances.

Three sides of this famous rock are precipitous. On the top is a large area, on the accessible part of which are 2 great ramparts of stone and within is the ruin of a stone building 10 yards long; the walls are dry but strong. Since it is certain that Vortigern, after his misfortunes, retired to the Snowdon hills and died not very remote from them, it is possible he selected this for his strong-hold as it is admirably adapted for that purpose and nearly fills the straight of the valley. Myrddin Ambrosius might have given to it the name of Emrys. A place close by styled Cell y Dewiniaid (*Cell of the Diviners*), allusive to the magicians of Vortigern's court, is another circumstance which favours the history of its supposed prophet.

From hence is a pleasant but short ride near the river to the village of Beddgelert, seated in a beautiful tract of meadows at the junction of 3 vales, near the conflux of the Glaslyn and the Colwyn which flows through Nant Colwyn, a vale that leads to Caernarfon. Its situation was the fittest in the world to inspire religious meditation amidst lofty mountains, wood and murmuring streams. The church is small, yet the loftiest in Eryri. The east window consists of 3 narrow slips. The roof is neat and there yet remains some very pretty fret-work. A side-chapel is supported by 2 neat pillars, and gothic arches. I could discover no tombs.

This church had been conventual, belonging to a priory of Augustines dedicated to St Mary. There is reason to suppose they might have been of that class which was called Gilbertines and consisted of both men and women who lived under the same roof but strictly separated from each other by a wall as I discovered a piece of ground near the church called Dôl-lleian (*Meadow of the Nun*).

Beddgelert had been the most ancient foundation in all the country except in Ynys Enlli. Tanner ascribes it to our last prince but it must have been long before his days, there being a recital of a charter for certain lands bestowed on it by Llywelyn the Great who began his reign in 1194. It was favoured in the same manner by others of the succeeding princes. The prior had besides an allowance of 50 cows and 22 sheep. The expenses of the house must have been large. It lay on the great road from England and West Wales into North Wales, and from Ireland and northern Wales into England. In order to enable this place to keep its usual hospitality after it had suffered in 1283, by a casual fire, Edward I most munificently repaired all the damages. About the year 1286, for the encouragement of other benefactors, Bishop Anian remitted to all such who were truly repentant of their sins 40 days of any penance inflicted on them.

# Chapter Nine

# Beddgelert to Clynnog

TO COMPLETE the mountain ramble as far as was in my power, I made an excursion from Beddgelert up a narrow vale. Ascended a steep road amidst a thin hanging wood and saw from the road multitudes of black cattle coming down from all parts on their way from a neighbouring fair. The vale expands and is watered by the Colwyn which flows from a small lake we passed, called Llyn Cader. Left on the right another ascent to Yr Wyddfa where its base extends to a considerable breadth and is far less steep than that on the side of Nant Peris. We soon reached the pretty lake, Llyn Cwellyn, noted for its char. Above the lake stood the house of Cae-uwch-llyn (*Field above the Lake*), from distant times the residents of the Quellyns (a family now extinct) who derived their name from the place. The mountains hereabouts approach near to each other. On the left, Mynydd Mawr forms a striking feature: its top is smooth but its front is formed into the most immense precipice, retiring inwards in a semicircular shape. Moel Eilio is another mountain of stupendous bulk, most regularly rounded and of a beautiful verdure. At Betws Garmon, a village with a church dedicated to St Germanus, the scene changes into a range of beautiful meadows watered by a rapid stream.

I here turned my back on the humble flats and resumed my former road till I had passed Llyn Cwellyn. Not far beyond that lake, I turned to visit Llyn y Dywarchen (*the Lake of the Sod*), long since celebrated by the hyperbolical pen of Giraldus for its insular erratica, its wandering island, as he calls it. That little lake is seated in the middle of a turbary and at this time actually exhibited the phenomenon recorded by a romantic historian. It had on it a floating island of an irregular shape and about 9 yards long. It appeared to be only a piece of the turbary, undermined by the water, torn off, and kept together by the close entangling of the roots

115

which form that species of ground. It frequently is set in motion by the wind, often joins its native banks and, as Giraldus says, cattle are frequently surprised on it and by another gale carried a short voyage from the shore.

Continue our journey to Drws-y-coed (*Pass of the Wood*), a pass towards Clynnog. It is bounded by vast mountains: on one side by Tal-y-mignedd, on the other by a great cleft of Mynydd Mawr. Some years ago here were considerable adventures for copper of the pyritous kind, and in the rocks were sometimes found some very thin laminae of the native metal. I was tempted here to exceed a little the limits of my Alpine tour for now the mountains descend fast from their majestic heights, growing less and less as they approach the Irish sea. My motive was to obtain a sight of two fine lakes called Llynnau Nantlle which form two handsome expanses with a very small distance between each. From hence is a noble view of Yr Wyddfa which terminates the view through the vista of Drws-y-coed. It is from this spot that Mr Wilson has favoured us with a view as magnificent as it is faithful. Few are sensible of this for few visit the spot.

Near these lakes Edward I, in the summer of 1284, resided for some days and from hence issued more than one of his edicts. I find some dated July 17th and 20th. Others are dated in the same year from Bangor, Caernarfon, Yr Wyddgrug and Estyn. One from Caernarfon is dated as late as October 22nd which shows what attention he paid to the establishment of government in his new dominions. The place he resided at here was called Baladeulyn, or the place where a river discharges itself from two lakes; but at present all memory is lost of the situation of the town, the traces of which might perhaps be still discovered by diligent search.

I returned by the same road and again reached Beddgelert where I made a coarse lodging. The evening was so fine that we were irresistibly tempted not to defer till morning our visit to Pont Aberglaslyn, a short walk from hence. The first part is along the narrow vale but in a very little time the mountains approach so close as to leave only room for the furious river to roll over its stony bed, above which is a narrow road, formed with incredible labour, impending over the water. The way seems to have been first cut out of the rock and then covered with great stones, as usual in several of our narrow passes. The scenery is the most magnificent that can be imagined. The mountains rise to a very uncommon height and oppose to us nothing but a broken series of precipices, one above the other, as high as the eye can reach. Here is very little appearance of vegetation yet in spots there is enough to tempt the poor goat to its destruction; for it will sometimes leap down to an alluring tuft of verdure where, without possibility of return, it must remain to perish after it has finished the dear-bought repast.

The bridge terminates the pass and consists of a single arch flung over a deep chasm from rock to rock. Above is a considerable cataract where the traveller at times may have much amusement in observing the salmon, in great numbers, make their efforts to surmount the weir. Near the place is a salmon fishery. Here had been a royal weir in the reign of Henry IV which was then rented by Robert ap Maredudd.

Opposite to Beddgelert is Moel Hebog. In a bog not far from that mountain was found a most curious brass shield which Mr Williams of Llanidan favoured me with a sight of. Its diameter was 2 feet 2 inches, the weight 4 pounds. In the centre was a plain umbo projecting above 2 inches. The surface of the shield was marked with 27 smooth concentric elevated circles and between each a depressed space, of the same breadth with the elevated parts, marked by a single row of smooth studs. The whole shield was flat and very limber. I cannot attribute this to the Welsh who seemed to despise every species of defensive armour.

On my return to Beddgelert, a stone by the road side was pointed out to me, by the name of the chair of Rhys Goch Eryri, the famous mountain bard, contemporary with Owain Glyndŵr. He was of the house of Hafod Garegog at the entrance into Traeth Mawr from whence he used to walk and, sitting on this stone, compose his poems. Amongst others is a satire on a fox for killing his favourite peacock. He died about the year 1420 and was interred in the holy ground of Beddgelert.

From Beddgelert I returned to Pont Aberglaslyn and soon reached Traeth Mawr, a large expanse of sands between the counties of Caernarfon and Meirionnydd, of most dangerous passage to strangers by reason of the tides which flow here with great rapidity. This forms the bottom of the Bae Ceredigion. In the year 1625, Sir John Wynn of Gwydir conceived the great design of gaining this tract, and a lesser called Traeth Bychan, from the sea, by an embankment. He implored the assistance of his illustrious countryman, Sir Hugh Middleton. Sir John's letter and Sir Hugh's reply will be the best account I can give of the affair; which was never carried into execution, as I imagine, for want of money:

"To the honoured Sir Hugh Myddleton, Knight, Baronet.

"Right worthy Sir, my good cousin, and one of the great honours of the nation, I understand of a great work that you have performed in the Isle of Wight, in gaining 2,000 acres from the sea. I may say to you what the Jews said to Christ - We have heard of thy great works done abroad, doe somewhat in thine own country.

"There are two washes in Merionethshire, whereon some part of my being lieth, called Traeth Mawr and Traeth Bychan, of a great extent of land, and entering into the sea by one issue, which is not a mile broad at full sea, and very shallow. The fresh currents that run into the sea are both vehement and great, and carry with them much sand; besides the southerly wind usually bloweth full to the haven's mouth, carrieth with it so much sand that it hath overwhelmed a great quantity of the ground adjacent. There, and also in the bordering countries, abundance of wood, brush and other materials to make mounds, to be had at a very cheap rate and easily brought to the place, which I hear they do in Lincolnshire to expel the sea. My skill is little and my experience none at all in such matters yet I ever had a desire to further my country in such actions as might be for their profit and leave a remembrance of my endeavours, but hindered with other matters I have only wished well and done nothing. Now being it pleased God to bring you into this country, I am to desire you to take a ride, the place not being above a day's journey from you; and if you do see the thing fit to be undertaken, I am content to adventure a brace of hundred pounds to join with you in the work.

"I have lead ore on my grounds great store, and other minerals near my house; if it please you to come hither, being not above two days' journey from you, you shall be most kindly welcome - it may be you shall find here that which will tend to your commodity and mine. If I did know the day certain when you would come to view Traeth Mawr, my son Owen Wynn shall attend you there and conduct you thence to my house. Concluding me very kindly to you, do rest, your loving cousin and friend,

"J. Wynn. Gwydir. 1st September 1625."

"Honourable Sir, I have received your kind letter. Few are the things done by me for which I give God the glory. It may please you to understand my first undertaking of public works was amongst my own, within less than a mile of the place where I had my first being, 24 or 25 years since, in seeking of coals for the town of Denbigh.

"Touching the drowned lands near your living, there are many things considerable therein. If to be gained, which will hardly be performed without great stones, which was plentiful at the weight, as well as wood; and great sums of money to be spent, not hundreds but thousands - and first of all his Majesty's interest must be got. As for myself, I am grown into years and full of business here at the mines, the river at London, and other places - my weekly charge being above 200 pounds; which maketh me very unwilling to undertake any other work; and the least of these, whether the drowned lands or mines, requireth a whole man with a large purse. Noble Sir, my desire is great to see you, which should draw me a far longer way; yet such are my occasions at this time here, for the settling of this great work, that I can hardly be spared one hour in a day. My wife being also here, I cannot leave here in a strange place. Yet my love to public works and desire to see you (if God permit) may another time draw me into those parts. So with my hearty commendations I commit you and all your good desires to God.

"Your assured loving cousin to command, Hugh Myddelton, Lodge, September 2nd 1625."

The view from the middle of the sands towards Eryri is most extravagantly wild. Mountain rises above mountain, exposing the most savage and barren aspect imaginable, ranked, precipitous and craggy. The Cnicht soars into a picturesque rocky cone and Yr Wyddfa rises in the background pre-eminent among its companions.

On quitting the sands, arrive in a tract of meadows sprinkled with insulated rocks and precipices. On the road observe some poor iron and groups of course crystals, the relics of an unprofitable mine adventure. The small town of Penmorfa lies at the head of these meadows. The church is dedicated to St Beuno and annexed to it is the chapel of Dolbenmaen. Here was interred that valiant knight Sir John Owen. Besides his monument is another small one to Sir William Morris of Clenennau who died August 11th 1622.

In former times this neighbourhood abounded with gentry. It lies in the hundred of Efionydd, in remote days possessed by 2 clans: one descended from Owain Gwynedd, Prince of Wales, and the other derived from Collwyn ap Tango. In the days I allude to, the feuds among the gentry filled the land with blood. This history of our country during that period is the history of revenge, perfidy and slaughter. This consideration induced Maredudd ap Ieuan, ancestor of the Wynnes of Gwydir, to quit his paternal country. "I had rather," says he, "fight with outlaws and thieves than with my own blood and kindred. If I live in my own house in Efionydd, I must either kill my own kinsmen or be killed by them."

During my stay at Penmorfa, I was desired to observe Dick Bach, a diminutive person who casually called there. He was servant to a neighbouring gentleman, was about the age of 30 and only 3 feet 11 inches high. He was pointed out to me only for the sake of describing his sister Mary Bach o Cwm-main, a well-proportioned fairy of 3 feet 4 inches. Her virtues are superior to her size: she brews, bakes, pickles, in short does every thing that the best housekeeper can do. Their parents live in the parts and have many children of the common stature of man but nature chose to sport in the formation of this little pair.

In the winter of 1694, the neighbourhood was remarkable for an amazing and noxious phenomenon. A mephites (or pestilential vapour) resembling a weak blue flame, arose during a fortnight or 3 weeks out of a sandy marshy tract called Morfa Bychan and crossed over a channel of 8 miles to Harlech. It set fire on that side to 16 ricks of hay and 2 barns. It infected the grass in such a manner that numbers of cattle, horses, sheep and goats died. Any great noise such as the sounding of horns or discharging of guns at once repelled it. It moved only by night and appeared at times, but less frequently, the following summer, after which this phenomenon ceased. It may possibly arise, as the editor of Camden conjectures, from a local casualty such as the fall of a flight of locusts in that spot, as really did in the sea near Aberdaron which, growing corrupt, might by the blowing of the wind direct the pest to a certain spot.

Passed by Ystumllyn and soon reach Cricieth, a poor borough town contributory to Caernarfon. Its castle is seated on a pretty hill jutting far into the sea and the isthmus crossed by 2 deep ditches. On each side of the entrance is a great round tower. The towers have so much the appearance of the architecture of Dolwyddelan castle that I entertain no doubt that this castle was founded by a Welsh prince and that its supposed founder, Edward I, did no more than case the towers. After the Conquest, Edward appointed William de Leybourn to be constable with a salary of 100 pounds a year, for which he was to maintain a garrison of 30 stout men (10 of whom were to be cross-bow men), one chaplain, one surgeon, one carpenter and one mason.

Our boasted countryman, Sir Hywel y Fwyall, was constable of this castle. He attended the Black Prince to the battle of Poitiers and, as we say, was the person who took the French king prisoner; but history bestows that honour on Denis de Morebeque, a knight of Artois.

Eight miles farther is Pwllheli. In my way cross over a pretty stream on a bridge of 3 arches at Llanystumdwy, a church and village in a pretty wooded bottom. Cross the little Afon Erch at Abererch, or the port of the coffin, near a church dedicated to St Cwrda. After another mile's ride reach Pwllheli, the best town in this country and the magazine of goods which supplies all this tract. It lies close on the shore and has a tolerable harbour for vessels of about 60 tons. The entrance is by a high rock called the Gimlet, a mile from land, to which it is joined by a range of sand-hills. This place was made a free borough by the Black Prince by charter dated the 12th year of this principality, at Caernarfon, in compliment to Nigel de Loryng or Lohareyn, one of the gentlemen of the bedchamber, on whom he had bestowed Pwllheli and Nefyn in consideration of his great service in Gascony and particularly at the battle of Poitiers. Pwllheli was to pay to Nigel 14 pounds a year and Nefyn 32.

From hence I took a ride about 5 miles inland to Garn Fadryn, a lofty rocky insulated hill noted for having been a stronghold of the sons of Owain Gwynedd, Rhodri and Maelgwn, to whom this part of the country belonged. The bottom, sides and top are filled with cells, oblong, oval or circular, once thatched or covered from the inclemency of the weather; many of them are pretty entire. The chieftains resided on the top. In times of invasion, the country, with the cattle, occupied the sides and bottom. The whole summit was surrounded by a wall still visible in many places. From the summit is an extensive view of the country, with the bay of Caernarfon on one side and that of Ceredigion on the other. Sarn Badrig is seen extending from Meirionnydd its dangerous length, nearly parallel to the shore of Llŷn. South Wales may be seen plainly, and in clear weather Ireland. In front, the whole tract of Eryri exhibits a most magnificent and stupendous barrier. At the foot of this hill is Madryn, formerly the seat of the Bodfels descended from Collwyn ap Tango.

From Pwllheli I continued my journey near the shore to Llanbedrog along the sides of that noble bay, St Tudwal's road, sheltered by 2 islands named from St Tudwal, sacred to whom was a chapel on the greater. Its present inhabitants are sheep, rabbits and, in the season, puffins.

In the promontory Penrhyn Du, one of the points of this bay, have been considerable adventurers for lead ore, and of late years attempts to drain the mines by means of a fire engine, but the expenses proved superior to the profits. A little beyond this is the bay of Porth Neigwl, called Hell's Mouth, dreaded by mariners.

In a small time I reached Aberdaron, a poor village at the very end of Llŷn, seated on a sandy bay beneath some high and sandy cliffs. It takes its name from the Afon Daron, a small rivulet which empties itself here. The mouth of the bay is guarded by 2 little islands, Ynys Gwylan Fawr and Bach, a security to the small craft of the inhabitants who are all fishermen.

From this port I once took boat for Ynys Enlli which lies abut 3 leagues to the west. The mariners seemed tinctured with the piety of the place; they had not rowed far but made a full stop, pulled off their hats and offered up a short prayer. Passing under the lofty mountain which forms one side, we put into a little sandy creek bounded by low rocks as is the whole level part. On landing, I found all this tract a very fertile plain, well cultivated and productive of every thing which the main land affords. The abbot's house is a large stone building inhabited by several of the natives; not far from it is a singular chapel or oratory, being a long arched edifice with an insulated stone altar near the east end. In this place one of the inhabitants reads prayers; all other offices are performed at Aberdaron.

The island is about 2 miles in circumference, contains few inhabitants and is rented from Lord Newborough. It was granted by Edward VI to his uncle Sir Thomas Seymour, and after his death to John Earl of Warwick. The late Sir John Wynn purchased it from the late reverend Dr Wilson of Newark. Its spiritual concerns are at present under the care of a single rustic and once afforded, during life, an asylum to 20,000 saints; after death, graves to as many of their bodies. Well therefore might it be called Insula Sanctorum (*Isle of Saints*). But I must observe with Mr Fuller that "it would be more facile to find graves in Bardseye for so many saints than saints for so many graves". Dubritius, archbishop of Caer-leon, almost worn out with age, resigned his see to St David and retired here. According to the best account, he died in 612 and was interred on the spot but in after times his body was removed to Llandaf. The slaughter of the monks of Bangor, about the year 607, is supposed to have contributed to the population of the island. Not only the brethren who escaped but numbers of other pious Britons fled hither to avoid the rage of the Saxons.

The time in which the religious house was founded is very uncertain; it was probably before the retreat of Dubritius for something of that kind must have occasioned him to give the preference to this place. It seems likely to have been a seat of the Culdees or Colidei, the first religious recluses of Great Britain, who sought islands and desert places in which they might in security worship the true God. It was an abbey dedicated to St Mary, undergoing the common fate of others at the dissolution.

The Welsh named the island Ynys Enlli (*island in the currents*) from the fierce current which rages particularly between it and the main land. The Vikings called it Bardsey, probably from the bards who retired here preferring solitude to the company of invading foreigners. There are plenty of fish round the island and abundance of lobsters. We re-embarked from the rocks on the opposite side of the island to that on which we landed.

Llŷn is a very extensive hundred, in general flat but interspersed with hills or rocks. The houses of the common people are very mean, made with clay, thatched and destitute of chimneys. Notwithstanding the laudable example of the gentry, the country is in an unimproved state, neglected for the sake of the herring-fishery. The chief produce is oats, barley and black cattle; I was informed that above 3,000 are annually sold out of these parts. Much oats, barley, butter and cheese are exported. The land is excellent for grazing but destitute of trees except about the houses of the gentry.

Descending into an extensive flat, reached Portin-llaen, a fine safe and sandy bay guarded on the west by a narrow headland jutting far into the sea. On part of it are the remains of very strong entrenchments, probably an outpost of the Romans who, as I shall have occasion to mention, had another between this place and Caernarfon.

Separated from this bay by a small headland is that of Nefyn and near to it a small town of the same name, a contributory borough to Caernarfon. This place had been bestowed on Nigel de Lohareyn by the Black Prince, in the 12th year of his principality, and made a free borough. He also gave it a grant of 2 fairs annually and a market on Sunday to which the inhabitants of that part of the Cwmwd Llŷn were obliged to resort.

Here Edward I, in 1284, held his triumph on the conquest of Wales and, perhaps to conciliate the affections of his new subjects, in imitation of our hero Arthur, held a round table and celebrated it with dance and tournament. The concourse was prodigious for not only the chief nobility of England but numbers from foreign parts graced the festival with their presence.

The custom is very ancient for it may be derived even higher than the days of Arthur. The Gauls also sat at their round tables and every knight had at his back a squire with his armour, in waiting. The first I apprehend to have been performed in those circular areas which we still meet in some parts of England, surrounded with a high mound, a ditch inside and 2 entrances opposite each other.

Ascend from Nefyn for a considerable way up the side of the high hill and, after a short ride on level ground, quit our horses in order to visit Nant Gwrtheyrn, (Vortigern's Valley), the immense hollow to which Vortigern is reported to have fled from the rage of his subjects and where it was said that he and his castle were consumed with lightning. Nennius places the scene in Carmarthenshire; but I believe that the historian not only mistakes the spot but even the manner of his death. His life had been profligate; the monks therefore were determined that he should not die the common death of all men and accordingly made him perish with signal marks of the vengeance of Heaven. Fancy cannot frame a place more fit for a retreat from the knowledge of mankind, or better calculated to inspire confidence of security from any pursuit. Embosomed in a lofty mountain, on two sides bounded by stony steeps on which no vegetables appear but the blasted heath and stunted gorse; the third side exhibits a most tremendous front of black precipice with the loftiest peak of the mountain Yr Eifl soaring above; and the only opening to this secluded spot is towards the sea (a northern aspect!) where that chilling wind exerts all its fury and half freezes during winter the few inhabitants. The glen is tenanted by three families who raise oats and keep a few cattle, sheep and goats, but seem to have great difficulty in getting their little produce to market.

Just above the sea is a high and verdant mount, natural but the top and sides worked by art; the first flatted, the sides marked with 8 prominent ribs from top to bottom. On this might have been the residence of the unfortunate prince, of which time has destroyed every other vestige. Till the beginning of the last century, a tumulus, of stone within and externally covered with turf, was to be seen here; it was known by the name of Bedd Gwrtheyrn; tradition having regularly delivered down the report of this having been the place of his interment. The inhabitants of the parish, perhaps instigated by their then minister, Mr Hugh Roberts, a person of curiosity, dug into the carn and found in it a stone coffin containing the bones of a tall man. This gives a degree of credibility to the tradition, especially as no other bones were found near the carn; nor were there any other tumuli on the spot: which affords a proof at least of respect to the rank of the person and that the place was deserted after the death of the royal fugitive, about the year 465.

After emerging out of this cheerless bottom, I found fresh and amazing matter of speculations. I got into a bwlch or hollow between 2 summits of Yr Eifl, a range that makes a most distinguished figure with the sugar-loaf points from various and distant parts of the country. They range obliquely and separate Llŷn from the hundred of Arfon, and jut into the sea near Nant Gwrtheyrn.

Across this hollow, from one summit of Yr Eifl to the other, extends an immense rampart of stones or perhaps the ruins of a wall which effectually blocked up the pass. On Yr Eifl is the most perfect and magnificent, as well as the most artfully constructed, Celtic post I ever beheld. It is called Tre'r Ceiri. This, which was the accessible side, was defended by 3 walls; the lowest is very imperfect, the next tolerably entire and has in it the grand entrance. This wall in one part points upwards towards the third wall, which runs round the edges at the top of the hill. The second wall unites with the first which runs into a point, reverts and joins the highest in a place where the hill becomes inaccessible. The facings on the 2 upper walls are very entire, especially that of the uppermost. They are lofty and exhibit from below a grand and extensive front. The space on the top is an irregular area; part is steep, part flat, in

124

most parts covered with heath, giving shelter to a few red grouse. The whole is almost filled with cells. To be seen to advantage, the station should be taken from the summit, about which the cells are very distinct and disposed with much art. About the middle is a square place fenced with stones, a sort of praetorium, surrounded with two rows of cells; numbers are also scattered about the plain and others again are contiguous to the wall along the inside.

The cells are mostly perfect, of various forms: round, oval, oblong, square. Some of the round were 15 feet in diameter. Of the oblong, 30 feet in length with long entrances regularly faced with stone. All of them, when inhabited, were well protected from the weather by roofs of thatch or sod.

The upper wall was in many places 15 feet high on the outside, and often 16 feet broad. It consisted of 2 parallel and contiguous parts, one higher than the other, serving as a parapet to the lower which seemed to have had its walk like that on the walls of Chester. There was in one place a cell in the thickness of the wall, or perhaps a sally-port, in part stopped by the falling-in of the stones.

I was determined to trace every species of fortress of this nature which lay in the neighbourhood. On descending from Tre'r Ceiri to the south, I very soon ascended Moel Carnguwch, a hill of conical form on the summit of which is a prodigious heap of stones, seemingly a shapeless ruin were it not for the appearance of certain facings of a central cell still remaining to prove that it had been a large tower and an outpost to the preceding place. These ruins are called by the country people Arffedoged y Gawres (*Apron-full of Stones Flung Down by the Giantess*).

I must remark that from Yr Eifl I saw several lesser eminences fortified in a manner nearly similar: Carn Fadryn before described, the hill of Boduan above Nefyn, Moel Bentyrch between Tre'r Ceiri and Penmorfa, Castell Gwgan and Pen y Gaer, all of which makes it probable that this country was the retreat of Britons to escape the first fury of the Saxon invaders.

After viewing Arffedoged-y-Gawres, I descended to the village and church of Llanaelhaearn, dedicated to St Aelhaearn (Saint with the Iron Eyebrow) from a legend too absurd to relate. Near it is a fine well, one much frequented for its reputed sanctity. Continue descending: on the right are the high conic hills of Gyrn Goch and Gyrn Ddu, the extremity of the long chain which extends obliquely from Yr Wyddfa.

# Chapter Ten

# Clynnog to Biwmares

REACH CLYNNOG, seated in a small grove near the shore on a plain foot of the hills. The church is the most magnificent structure of its kind in North Wales, built in the form of a cross. The length from east to west is about 138 feet, from north to south 70. The monuments are few: one to William Glynn de Lleuar with his figure and those of his wife and children; another to his son-in-law George Twistleton and his wife of Lleuar. I imagine him to be the same who had the honour of beating and making prisoner the gallant Sir John Owen.

Adjoining to the church is the chapel of St Beuno. The passage to it is a narrow vault covered with great flat stones and of far greater antiquity than either church or chapel which seem nearly coeval. Votaries were wont to have a great faith in him and did not doubt but that by means of a night's lodging on his tomb a cure would be found for all diseases. I myself once saw on it a feather bed on which a poor paralytic from Meirionnydd had lain the whole night after undergoing ablution in the neighbouring holy well.

After assuming the monastic habit, Beuno here founded a convent in 616. Cadfan, King of North Wales, was his great patron and promised him much land. Cadfan's son Cadwallan performed the promise and received from the saint a golden sceptre worth 60 cows. The land was later claimed in behalf of a little infant and, his title proving good, the king refused either to give other land in lieu or to resign the present. Beuno cursed him and went away but was appeased by Gwrddeint, first cousin to the king, who overtook him and gave the town of Clynnog for ever to God and St Beuno, for his own soul's sake and that of the wicked Cadwallan. Its revenues at the dissolution are not recorded but they must at one time have been very great; many of the kings and first people of the country appear on the list of benefactors. At present there are, I believe, no sort of revenues to keep this venerable pile from falling into ruin. The offerings of calves and lambs which happen to be born with Nod Beuno, or mark of St Beuno, a certain natural mark in the ear, have not entirely ceased. The little money resulting from the sacred beasts, or casual offerings, is either applied to the relief of the poor or in aid of repairs.

A very uncommon cromlech may be seen on the tenement of Bachwen about half a mile from this place. At 30 paces distant is an upright stone placed, as is supposed. to mark the limits of approach to the people while the rites were performing by the Druid-priest.

The distance from Clynnog to Caernarfon is 10 miles,; the mountains recede gradually from the sea so as to leave a considerable tract of level ground as we approach the capital of the county. The road is excellent and the greatest part has the merit of being made at the expense of the parish. The shore is low, gravelly or sandy and forms one side of the bay of Caernarfon.

Cross the Llyfni, a rapid stream flowing out of Llyn Nantlle. I heard here of a strong camp called Carreg y Dinas of which I find this note in the manuscript travels of the late ingenious Dr Mason of Cambridge. He mentions it as being placed upon the isthmus of the Llyfni opposite to the house of Lleuar. The 3 sides to the river are very steep; the 4th is defended by 2 fosses and 2 banks, made chiefly of stone, especially the inner one which is 6 yards high. In the middle is a mount, possibly the ruins of a tower. The entrance is at the east end between the ends of the banks.

About 3 miles, turn to the left to visit Dinas Dinlle: a vast mount of gravel and sand on the verge of a great marsh, upon the shore. On the top is a large area, surrounded by an amazing agger seemingly formed by the earth scooped out of the summit. Within are the remains of foundations of buildings of an oblong form constructed with earth and round stones, and in one part is a tumulus of the same materials. The waves have made great depredations and worn one side into a cliff. I attribute this fortress to the Romans and am informed that coins have been found here, among which was one of Alectus. The Romans might possibly be induced to form this post to secure a landing place for any necessaries the country might want. The entrance into the port of Segontium is often very difficult even at present; much more so in the earlier times of navigation. There may be another of the same kind for I find in the old maps both of Saxton and Speed the name Caer Arianrhod a little lower down at the mouth of the Llyfni. By the addition of the word Caer, it must have been a fortified place.

When I made my visit to Dinas Dinlle, I was under the guidance of a worthy friend and learned antiquary, the Reverend Richard Farrington (now deceased). He conducted me to his residence at Dinas Dinoethwy about 4 miles distant. In the way, he showed me Dinas y Prif (*The Post of the Chieftain*), a small camp about 44 yards square. Each corner is elevated above the ramparts and inside are foundations of some stone buildings. By the name, it might have been the summer station of the Roman commander-in- chief resident at Segontium.

From Dinas I visited Glynllifon, a house built by the late Sir John Wynn, seated near the little Afon Llifon which issues from the Cilgwyn mountain. Cilmyn Troed-ddu or Cilmyn with a black foot, one of the 15 tribes of North Wales and nephew to Merfyn Frych, Prince of Wales, slain in 841, had his residence on this spot. From him are descended the family of the Glynns who took their name from the place. A ridiculous legend tells you that Cilmin's leg became discoloured by escaping from a demon whose books he had assisted a magician to steal. In leaping over a brook which was to be the limit of the pursuit, Cilmin's left leg plunged into the water and assumed its sable dye.

Continue my journey on a turnpike road. At Bontnewydd cross the Gwyrfai which flows from Llyn Cwellyn and soon after cross the Seiont to reach Caernarfon.

This town is justly the boast of North Wales for the beauty of situation and, above all, the grandeur of the castle, the most magnificent badge of our subjection. The place sprang from the ruin of the ancient Segontium but does not owe its name to Edward I as is generally supposed. Giraldus Cambrensis mentions it in his journey of the year 1188 and Llywelyn the Great dates from it a charter in the year 1221. I greatly suspect the Caernarfon of those times to have been no other than the ancient Segontium which the Welsh had called Caer yn Arfon (*the stronghold opposite to Ynys Môn*) since Celtic times. But the present town was in all probability a creation of our conqueror. Edward undertook this great work immediately after his conquest of the country in 1282 and completed the fortifications and castle before 1284; his queen, on April 25th of that year, brought forth within its walls Edward, first Prince of Wales of the English line. It was built within the space of one year by the labour of the peasants and at the cost of the chieftains of the country, on whom the conqueror imposed the hateful task. It is probably that many of the materials were brought from Segontium, the old Caernarfon. Tradition says that much of the lime-stone was brought from Twr Celyn in Ynys Môn and the grit-stone from Faenol in this county. The Menai greatly facilitated the carriage from both places.

I can discover no more than 2 instances of this place having suffered by the calamities of war. In the great insurrection of the Welsh under Madog, in 1294, they surprised the town during the time of the fair and put many English to the sword. Captain Swanley, a parliamentarian officer, took the town in 1644, made 400 prisoners and got a great quantity of arms, ammunition and pillage. The royalists afterwards repossessed themselves of the place. Lord Byron was appointed governor but was besieged by General Mytton in 1646 and yielded the place on the most honourable terms. In 1648. the General himself and Colonel Mason were besieged in its by Sir John Owen. Hearing that Colonels Carter and Twistleton were on the march to relieve the place, Sir John drew a party from the siege to attack them on the way. The parties met near Llandegai. Sir John was defeated and made prisoner; after that all North Wales submitted to the parliament.

Caernarfon is destitute of manufactures but has a brisk trade with London, Bristol, Liverpool and Ireland for the several necessaries of life. It is the residence of numbers of genteel families and contains several very good houses. Plâs Pulesdon is remarkable for the fate of its first owner, Sir Roger de Pulesdon, a distinguished favourite of Edward I who was appointed sheriff and keeper of the county of Ynys Môn in 1284. He was directed in 1294 to levy a subsidy for the French war. This was a tax the Welsh had never been accustomed to; they took up arms and hanged de Pulesdon and several of his people. This was a signal for a general insurrection. Madog, a relation of the late Prince Llywelyn, headed the people of this country. Edward marched against them in person and with great difficulty reduced the country to submit again to his yoke.

The mother church of Caernarfon is about half a mile southeast of the town, it is called Llanbeblig, being dedicated to St Peblig or Publicius, according to our historians son of Macsen Wledig (Maximus the ruler) and his wife Helen, daughter of Euddaf.

Near the step bank of the river Seiont, at a small distance from the castle, is an ancient Roman fort. On 2 sides the walls are pretty entire; one is 74 yards long and the other 64. The height 10 feet 8 inches and the thickness 6 feet. Much of the facing is taken away which discovers the peculiarity of Roman masonry. At a small distance above this, and about a quarter of a mile from Menai, is the ancient Segontium. It forms an oblong seemingly about 6 acres placed on the summit of rising ground and sloping down on every side. It is now divided by a public road but in several parts are vestiges of walls and in one place appears the remnant of a building made with tiles and plastered with very hard and smooth mortar.

*Llanfair Church and Plasnewydd*

The traveller who wishes to visit Snowdon from this town may have a very agreeable ride. After crossing the Gwyrfai, at Pont y Betws about 4 miles and a half from Caernarfon, he will find about the village of Betws Garmon, or Is-Gwyrfai, a beautiful cascade fronting him as he passes up a valley. He will go under Moel Eilio, a noble mountain of a stupendous bulk clothed with a smooth green turf and most regularly rounded. He will pass on the right near Castell Cidwm, said by Mr Rowlands to be one of the guards to the entrance to Snowdon. It is a great rock, which I did not ascend so cannot certify whether it had any works like those of other Celtic posts. The lake Cwellyn here almost fills the valley, a water famous for its char which are taken in nets in the first winter months and after that season retire to its inaccessible depths. In former times, this water was called Llyn y Torlennydd from the steepness of its banks. Above on the right side of the lake soars the magnificent Mynydd Mawr, smooth on the top but the sides receding inwards in a semicircular form exhibiting a tremendous precipice. Soon after this, the vale expands; Yr Wyddfa appears in full view. The traveller will pass by Llyn y Cader and join in my former tour at Beddgelert.

From Caernarfon I crossed the ferry to Tal-y-Foel in Ynys Môn. The Menai is here 2 miles broad. Had a view of Abermenai, the very narrow passage into the port of Caernarfon rendered more dangerous by the sands both within and without. Abermenai has its ferry and is one of the 5 over this strait. They were originally the property of the crown of England till Henry VIII granted all of them to Richard Gifford, one of the sewers of his chamber, who again set them to William Bulkely, but every one has since been transferred to other hands.

I soon reached Newborough (or more properly Rhosfair, the Welsh name) about 3 miles from the shore. Here had been one of the residences of our princes. In Mr Rowlands' time, the foundation of the Llys, or palace, was to be seen a little to the south of the church. Newborough now subsists by a manufacture of mats and rhofir morhesg ropes, made of sea reed-grass. Queen Elizabeth widely prohibited the extirpation of this plant to prevent having half the parish buried in the unstable sands by the rage of the tempests. Such is the case with Llanddwyn; almost the whole is at present covered with sand-hills. In the reign of Henry VIII it was one of the richest prebends in the cathedral of Bangor. Its wealth arose not from the real fertility of the place but from the superstition of the common people: from pilgrimages to crosses, relics, holy wells, ordeals and divination from fishes.

On the peninsular are the ruins of the church, dedicated to St Dwynwen, daughter of Brychan, one of the holy Colidei or primitive

Christians of Britain.

From Newborough, I several years ago made an excursion to Aberffro, about 7 miles to the north, in search of another palace of our ancient princes. They took one of their titles from this place, Princeps de Aberffro, which preceded that of Dominus de Snowdon. I crossed at low water the arm of the sea called Malltraeth and rode by the church of Llangadwaladr, said to have been founded by Cadwaladr, last king of the Britons, and made one of the sanctuaries of the island.

About a mile or 2 farther reach the site of the princely residence. It is now reduced to a few poor houses seated on the Afon Ffraw near a small bay. Not a vestige is to be seen of its former boast. It was the chief seat of our princes and one of the 3 courts of justice for the principality. Here was always kept one of the 3 copies of the ancient code of laws, another at Dinefwr in Carmarthenshire, and the third was kept by the doctors of laws for their constant use. This place was of great antiquity, being one of the 3 fixed on by Rhodri Mawr about the year 870 for the residence of his successors. In 962 it was ravaged by the Irish.

I must not pass unnoticed the celebrated stone of Maen Morddwyd (the stone of the thigh), now well secured in the wall of Llanidan church. In old times it was so constant to one place that, let it be carried ever so far, it would be sure of returning at night. Hugh Lupus, Earl of Chester, determined to subdue its loco-motive facilities, fastened it with iron chains to a far greater stone and flung it into the sea; but, to the astonishment of all beholders, it was found the next morning in its usual place.

I now enter on classical ground and the pious seats of the ancient Druids: the sacred groves, the altars and monumental stones. A slight mention of what I saw must content my read, who is referred to the works of the celebrated and learned Mr Henry Rowlands, the former rector of the place, and to those of my friend the late reverend Dr Borlase who hath added fresh illustrations of these obscure remains.

At Tre-Dryw, or the habitation of the Arch-Druid, I met with the mutilated remains described by Mr Rowlands. His Bryn Gwyn is a circular hollow 180 feet in diameter surrounded by an immense agger of earth and stones. It has only a single entrance. This is supposed to have been the grand consistory of the druidical administration. Not far from it was one of the Gorseddau, now dispersed but once consisted of a great copped heap of stones on which sat aloft a Druid instructing the surrounding people. Here were also the relics of a circle of stones with the cromlech in the midst but all extremely imperfect. Two of the stones are very large; one, which serves at present as part of the end of a house, is 12 feet 6 inches high and 8 feet broad, and another 11 feet high and 23 feet in girth. Some lesser stones yet remain. It is the conjecture of Mr Rowlands that the whole of these remains were surrounded with a circle of oaks and formed a deep and sacred grove.

The shore near Porth-amel is famed for being the place where Suetonius landed and put an end in this island to the Druid reign. There are no traces of any Roman works left in this country. Their stay was so short that they had not time to form any thing permanent.

About 3 miles from this place is Moel-y-Don ferry. The army of Edward I in 1282 made here an attempt fatal to many a gallant man. He landed his forces in the island and, after reducing to obedience the few inhabitants who had not taken the oath of fealty to him, built a bridge of boats near this place; some say at the very spot where Agricola passed. The Welsh, aware of his design, flung up entrenchments to secure the entrance into the mountains. Luke de Tany, a commander who had lately come from Gascony with a number of Gascon and Spanish troops, rashly passed over the unfinished bridge at low water, in contempt perhaps of the enemy. The flowing tide cut off access to the nearest part of the bridge and the Welsh suddenly rushed on them with hideous shouts, slew numbers and forced the remainder into the sea. On this occasion perished Tany himself, Roger Clifford the younger, 13 knights, 17 young gentlemen and 200 soldiers. William Latimer alone escaped by the goodness of his horse which swam with him to the bridge.

Porthaethwy, the most general ferry into Ynys Môn, is immediately below the church of Llandysilio. The passage of cattle at this place is very great. It is computed that the island sends forth annually from 12,000 to 15,000 heads and multitudes of sheep and hogs. It is also computed that the remaining stock of cattle is 30,000. My same authority says that in 1770 upwards of 90,000 bushels of corn were exported. He reckons only barley, rye and oats but I have seen most incomparable wheat growing on the island.

The Danes frequently invaded Ynys Môn and, between the years 969 and 972, Godfryd the son of Harold subdued the whole island.

I continued my ride near the Menai which now opens considerably. The opposite limits are inexpressibly beautiful, lofty and finely clothed with hanging woods. Bangor is a magnificent bay bounded by the great promontory Penmaenmawr and the vast Llandudno, apparently insulated. The estuary of the river Conwy flows at its bottom between those noble headlands. This prospect is seen to best advantage from the Green near the castle of Biwmares from whence may be also seen Ynys Seiriol, the fortress itself, Baron Hill and its elegant improvements, and

Red Hill, the house of Mr Sparrow.

The town of Biwmares is, as the name implies, pleasantly seated on a low land at the water's edge; it is neat and well built, and one street is very handsome. Edward I created the place. After founding the castles of Caernarfon and Conwy, he discovered that it was necessary to put another curb on my headstrong countrymen. He built this fortress in 1295 and fixed on a marshy spot near the chapel of St Meugan giving him opportunity of forming a great fosse round the castle and of filling it with water from the sea. He also cut a canal to permit vessels to discharge their lading beneath the walls. Within this century, there were iron rings affixed to the walls for the purpose of mooring the ships or boats.

Edward's three castles differ in form. This has least claim to beauty, not having the height or elegance of Caernarfon or Conwy. The exterior walls are guarded by ten strong towers. Within is a square of 190 feet. The entrance faces the sea and near it is a long narrow advanced work called the Gunners Walk.

The first governor was Sir William Pickmore, a Gascon knight appointed by Edward I. There was a constable of the castle and a captain of the town. The first had an annual fee of 40 pounds, the last of 12 pounds 3 shillings and 4 pence, and the porter of the gate of Biwmares had 9 pounds 2 shillings and 6 pence. 24 soldiers were allowed for the guard of the castle and town at 4 pence a day to each.

The castle was extremely burdensome to the country. Quarrels were frequent between the garrison and the country people. In the time of Henry VI, a bloody fray happened in which Dafydd ap Ifan ap Hywel of Llwydiarth, and many others, were slain. From the time of Sir Rowland Villeville, alias Brittayne, reputed base son of Henry VII and constable of the castle, the garrison was withdrawn till the year 1642 when Thomas Cheadle, deputy to the Earl of Dorset, then constable, put into it men and ammunition. In 1643, Thomas Bulkeley, soon after created Lord Bulkeley, succeeded. His son, Colonel Richard Bulkeley, and several gentlemen of the country, held it for the king till June 1646 when it surrendered on honourable terms to General Mytton who made Captain Evans his deputy governor. In 1653 the annual expense of the garrison was 1703 pounds.

Edward I, when he built the town, surrounded it with walls, made it a corporation and endowed it with great privileges and lands to a considerable value. He removed the ancient freeholders, by exchange of property, into other countries. Henllys, near the town, was the seat of Gweirydd ap Rhys Goch, one of the 15 tribes, and of his posterity till this period, when Edward removed them to Bodelwyddan, Fflint. It sends one member to parliament. Its first representative was Maurice Gruffudd who sat in the 7th year of Edward VI.

There is very good anchorage for ships in the bay which lies before the town and has 7 fathoms water even at the lowest ebb. Vessels often find security here in hard gales. The town has no trade of any kind yet has its customhouse for the casual recaption of goods. The ferry lies near the town and is passable even at low-water. It was granted a charter in the 4th of Queen Elizabeth. It appears that the people of Biwmares payed annually 30 shillings into the exchequer for the privilege of a ferry but by this order it seems that the king was to find the boat. After passing the channel, the distance over the sands to Aber, the point the passenger generally makes for, is 4 miles. The sands are called Traeth Lafan, and Wylofain, (*the Place of Weeping*), from the shrieks and lamentations of the inhabitants when it was overwhelmed by the sea in the days of Helig ap Clunog.

At a small distance from the town, on the shore, stand the remains of Llan-faes or The Friers. It was founded by Prince Llywelyn ap Iorwerth and, according to tradition, over the grave of his wife Joan, daughter of King John, who died in 1237 and was interred on the spot. Here also were interred a son of a Danish king, Lord Clifford and many barons and knights who fell in the Welsh wars. The religious were Franciscans, or minor friars. I am informed that on the farm of Cremlyn Monach, once the property of the friary, is cut on a great stone the effigy of its patron St Francis and that his head is also cut on the stone of a wall in a street of Biwmares, to which all passengers were to lay their respects under pain of a forfeit.

About the year 818, a bloody battle was fought near Llan-faes. Neither occasion or parties are mentioned but by the text (Powel, 24) I guess it to have been between Egbert King of the West Saxons , and the Welsh; for the former carried his arms into all parts of North Wales in the reign of Merfyn Frych.

A little farther is Castell Aberlleiniog, a small square fort with the remains of a little round tower at each corner. In the middle once stood a square tower. A fosse surrounds the whole. A hollow way is carried quite to the shore and at its extremity is a large mound of earth designed to cover the landing. The castle was founded in 1098 by Hugh Lupus Earl of Chester and Hugh the Red Earl of Shrewsbury when they made an invasion. This fort was garrisoned so lately as the time of Charles I when it was kept for the parliament by Sir Thomas Cheadle but was taken by Colonel Robinson in 1645 or 6.

About a mile farther I visited the Priory of Penmon, placed like the former on the shore. The remains are the ruinous refectory and the church; part of the last is in present use. Within is a small monument informing us that Sir Thomas Wilford of Ildington in Kent (one of whose daughters married Sir Richard Bulkeley) died January 25th 1645.

About a mile from the shore is Ynys Seiriol. The first recluses of this island, according to Giraldus, were hermits or whom (as usual) he tells a superstitious tale that they were plagued with swarms of mice whenever they disagreed. At the dissolution the revenues were valued at 47 pounds 15 shillings 3 pence, granted in the 6th of Queen Elizabeth to John More.

Ynys Seiriol is about a mile long and bounded by precipices except on the side opposite Penmon, and even there the ascent is very steep. The land slopes greatly from the summit to the edge of the precipices. During part of summer the whole swarms with birds of passage. The slope on the side is animated with puffin auks, *British Zoology* index number 232, which incessantly squall round you, alight and disappear into their burrows, or come out, stand erect and gaze at you in a most grotesque manner, then take flight and either perform their evolutions about you or seek the sea in search of food. They appear first about the 5th or 10th of April but quite the place, almost to a bird, twice or thrice before they settle. Their first employ is in the forming of burrows, which falls to the share of the males who are so intent on the business as to suffer themselves at that time to be taken by the hand. Some few save themselves the trouble of forming holes and will dispossess the rabbits who, during the puffin season, retire to the other side of the island.

They lay one white egg. Males as well as females perform the office of sitting, relieving each other when they go to feed. The young are hatched in the beginning of July. The parents have the strongest affection for them but this affection ceases at the time of re-migration, about the 11th of August. They then go off, to a single bird, and leave behind the unfledged young of the later hatches as prey to the peregrine falcon which watched the mouth of the holes for their appearance, compelled as the must soon be by hunger to come out.

The foot of these birds is sprats, or sea-weeds, which makes them excessively rank, yet the young are pickled and preserved by spices, and by some people much admired.

The channel between Ynys Seiriol and Ynys Môn has produced some very uncommon fish. The Biwmares shark, the morris, and the trifurcated hake are new species taken in this sea. The new mussel, called the umbilicated, is also frequently dredged up in the neighbourhood of this isle.

The Smirnium Olusatrum, or Alexander's, almost covers the south-west end of the island and is greedily eaten (boiled) by sailors who are just arrived from long voyages. The Iris Foctidissima, or stinking Gladwin, is common about the square tower and is frequently made into a poultice with oatmeal and used by the country people with success in the quinsy.

# Chapter Eleven

# Biwmares to Conwy

**I RETURNED** to Biwmares and from thence visited Baron-Hill, the seat of Lord Bulkeley, placed at the head of an extensive lawn sloping down to the town, backed and winged by woods, which are great embellishments to the country. The founder of Baron-Hill was Sir Richard Bulkeley, a most distinguished personage. He built it in 1618.

I proceeded on my journey and at Trefor passed by a great and rude cromlech with the ruins of others adjacent. Reach Plas Gwyn, the seat of my friend Paul Panton in right of his first wife Jane, daughter of William Jones. The house was built by Mr Jones and may be reckoned among the best of the island.

From Plas Gwyn I made an excursion to Traeth Coch, a large bay covered with firm sand which, on the west side, has so large a mixture of shells as to be used as a manure in all parts of the island within reasonable distance. Near the shore on the east side, about 3 miles from Plas Gwyn, are 2 rounded mounts on each side of a deep gully leading towards Llanddona church. These seem to have been the work of the Danes, cast up to protect their vessels in their plundering excursions, a calamity to which it appears, from the writing of our poets, this island was much subject.

Above Llanddona is a high hill called Bwrdd Arthur (*Arthur's Table*). The true name was probably Din, or Dinas Sylwy, for a church immediately beneath bears that of Llanfihangel Dinsylwy. On the top of it is a great Celtic post surrounded by a double row of rude stones with their sharp points uppermost and in some parts the ramparts are formed of small stones. In the area are vestiges of oval buildings; the largest is formed with 2 rows of flat stones. It is worth while to ascend this hill for the sake of the vast prospect, an intermixture of sea, rock and alps, most savagely great.

I descended to the church of Llaniestyn, remarkable for the tomb of its tutelar saint St Estyn or Iestyn, son of Geraint, a worthy knight of Arthur's round table, slain by the Saxons at the siege of London.

Another excursion was to Penmynydd, about 2 miles south of Plas Gwyn, once the residence of the ancestors of Owain Tudor, second husband to Catherine of France, queen dowager of Henry V. The match, important in its consequences, restored the Brythonic races of princes to this kingdom.

No more our long-lost Arthur we bewail:
All-hail, ye genuine kings; Britannia's issue, hail!

About a mile farther I visited Tre-garnedd, a farm-house in the parish of Llangefni, once the site of the great Ednyfed Fychan. Directly descended from him were Henry VII and VIII, Edward VI, Queen Mary and Queen Elizabeth, and every crowned head in England ever since, besides heroes not less illustrious in their degree. The name of this place is taken from an immense carnedd, or heap of stones, surrounded with great upright stones in an adjacent field. It seems to have beneath it passages formed on the sides and tops with flat stones or flags. These were the repositories of the dead.

A few years ago, beneath a carnedd similar to that at Tre-garnedd, was discovered on a farm called Bryncelli-ddu, near the seat of Sir Nicholas Bayley, a passage 3 feet wide, 4 feet 2 or 3 inches high, and about 19 feet and a half long which led into a room about 3 feet in diameter and 7 in height. In the middle was an artless pillar of stone, 4 feet 8 inches in circumference. This supports the roof which consists of one great stone near 10 feet in diameter. Along the sides of the room was, if I may be allowed the expression, a stone bench on which were found human bones which fell to dust almost at a touch; it is probable that the bodies were originally placed on the bench. There are proofs that it was customary with the Gauls to place their dead in that form in cells but they added to the head of each body a stone weapon which served as a pillar, but nothing of the kind was discovered in this sepulchre. The diameter of this incumbent carnedd is from 90 to 100 feet. This seems to be that which Mr Rowland takes notice of in his 'Mona Antiqua'.

I must not omit mention of the great patriarch of Tregaian, a chapelry of this parish, who lived in the year 1580 and died at the age of 105; his name was William ap Hywel ap Iorwerth. He had by his first wife 22 children, by his second 10, by his third 4, and by his 2 concubines 7; in all 43. His eldest son was 84 in 1581, his eldest daughter 72 and his youngest son then only 2 years and a half old. He was small of stature, of a cheerful convivial temper but spare in his diet, living mostly on milk.

He passed his time in rural employments, and at his leisure in fishing and fowling, and preserved his memory and senses to the last.

I returned to Plas Gwyn and from thence crossed Traeth Coch to the western horn of the bay called Castell-mawr, a small cape, flat at the top and joined to the land by a small isthmus. It is composed of lime-stone, which is carried to distant parts in small vessels that lie in a small channel near the rock and by their numbers frequently enliven the view. Roman coins have been found in this neighbourhood but there are no vestiges of there having been any station. On the shore beyond, I saw vast blocks of black marble filled with shells, corolloids and fungitae.

Proceed near the shore. On the left are the woods of Llugwy. Not far from the road is a most stupendous cromlech of a rhomboid form. The greatest diagonal is 17 feet 6 inches, the lesser 15, the thickness 3 feet 9. Its height from the ground is only 2 feet; it was supported by several stones. The Welsh, who ascribe every thing stupendous to our famous Welsh king, called it Arthur's quoit. In the woods are some druidical circles, nearly contiguous to each other.

Cross Traeth Llugwy and soon ride over Traeth Dulas, likewise dry at low water. It runs about a mile and a half deep into the country and is frequented by small vessels which take off the oats and butter of these parts. Off the mouth is a small island. Near this place, Caswallon Law-hîr kept his llŷs or court. He made a grant of lands and several privileges to this church, among which was that of a Nawddfa or sanctuary.

From hence I visited Trysglwyn mountain, on part of which (called Parys mountain, probably from a Robert Parys who was chamberlain of North Wales in the reign of Henry IV) is the most considerable body of copper ore perhaps ever known. The external aspect of the hill is extremely rude and rises into enormous rocks of coarse white quartz. The ore is lodged in a basin or hollow and has on one side a small lake on whose waters, distasteful as those of Avernus, no bird is known to alight. The whole aspect of this tract has, by the mineral operations, assumed a most savage appearance. Suffocating fumes of the burning heaps of copper arise in all parts and extend their baneful influence for miles around. In the adjacent parts vegetation is nearly destroyed; even the mosses and lichens of the rocks have perished and nothing seems capable of resisting the fumes but the purple Melic grass which flourishes in abundance.

I have little doubt but that the ore had been worked in a very distant period. Vestiges of the ancient operations appear in several parts, carried on by trenching and by heating the rocks intensely then suddenly pouring on water so as to cause them to crack or scale. Pieces of charcoal were also found which prove that wood was made use of for that purpose.

Copper is quarried out of the bed in vast masses, is broken into small pieces, and the most pure part is sold raw at the rate of about 3 pounds to 6 pounds per ton, or sent to the smelting-houses of the respective companies to be melted into metal. An idea of the wealth of these mines may be formed by considering that the Macclesfield company, Messrs Roe and Co, have had at once 14,000 tons of ore upon bank and Mr Edward Hughes 30,000. The more impure ore is also broken to about the size of hen's eggs but, in order to clear from it the quantity of sulphur with which it abounds, as well as other adventitious matter, it must undergo the operation of burning. Within these few years, attempts are made to preserve the sulphur from flying away from the kilns. That is done by flues made of brick, whose tops are in the form of a Gothic arch many scores of feet in length. One end of these opens into the beds of copper which are to be burnt. Those beds are set on fire by a very small quantity of coal, for all the rest is affected by its own phlogiston. The sulphurous particles strike against the roofs of the flues and fall to the bottom as finest brimstone which is melted into what is called in the shops stone brimstone.

The beds of copper thus piled for burning are of vast extent. Some contain 400 tons of ore, others 2,000. The first require 4 months to be completely burnt, the last near 10 months. Thus burnt, it is carried to proper places to be dressed, or washed, and made merchantable.

These works have added greatly to the population of the island for about 1,500 persons are employed who, with their families, are supposed to make near 8,000 persons getting their bread from these mines. The little village of Amlwch, the port of the place, is increasing fast and the market grows considerable. The port is no more than a great chasm between 2 rocks, running far into land, and dry at low water; into which sloops run and lie secure to receive their lading.

From Parys mountain I visited the north-west parts of the island and passed over a sandy plain country fertile in grain. See to the right the Middle Mouse and farther on is the third small isle of that name, called the West Mouse. Between these is Cemlyn Bay where there is a safe anchorage for small vessels. Not far from hence I saw the noted quarry of marble common to this place, to some parts of Italy and to Corsica, and known in the shops by the name of Verde di Corsica. It is a compound species of marble, apt to be intersected by small cracks or by asbestine veins, therefore incapable of taking a high polish. This quarry lies on the lands of Monachty in the parish of Llanfair-yng-Nghornwy, and is found again in Ynys off this parish. Neither the quarry nor the asbestos is at

*Holyhead Church*

present in use. The ancients set a high value on the last, a price equal to that of pearls. They wove napkins of it and at great feasts divested themselves (in order to clean them) to fling them into the fire, from which they returned unhurt and with improved lustre. They likewise made of it shrouds for the bodies of great men before they were placed on the funeral pile, and by that means preserved their ashes pure from those of the wood.

From Carreg-Llwyd I made an attempt to sail to the Skerries, called in Welsh Ynysoedd y Moelrhoniaid or the Isle of Seals, distant about a league from this place and about half a league from the nearest part of Ynys Môn. A turbulent sea made us return with speed. The island is very rocky but affords food for a few sheep, rabbits and puffins. The light-house placed on it about the year 1730 is of great use to ships sailing between Ireland and the ports of Chester and Liverpool.

Let me record that a few years ago were found, on a farm called Ynys y Gwyddyl in the parish of Llanfflewin, 4 miles east of Carreg-Llwyd, 3 golden bracelets and a golden Bulla in high preservation. Two of the former I purchased and preserved as curious memorials of the residence of the Romans in ancient Mona.

From Carreg-Llwyd I rode to Caergybi, about 11 or 12 miles distant. The town is small but greatly resorted to by passengers to and from the kingdom of Ireland, and is the station of the packet boats, 5 of which are in constant employ, are stout vessels and well manned. St Gybi is said to have founded a small monastery here about the year 380. Maelgwn Gwynedd, who began his reign about the year 580, is said to have founded a college here. Others assert that the founder was his contemporary, Hwfa ap Cynddelw, Lord of Llys Llifon in this island and one of the 15 tribes of North Wales.

Near the church of St Gybi stood, in old times, a chapel called Eglwys y Bedd (*Church of the Grave*) and Capel Llan y Gwyddel (*Chapel of the Irishmen*). Sirigi, a king of the Irish Picts, invaded the country and was slain by Caswallon Law Hir (*Caswallon the Long-handed*) who reigned about the year 440. Sirigi was canonised by his countrymen and had in this chapel a shrine in high repute for many miracles. This place had distinct revenues from the collegiate church. At length it fell into ruin and was disused for ages. In removing the rubbish not many years ago, a stone coffin was found with bones of a stupendous size; but we must not suppose these to have been the relics of Sirigi as they had been carried away by some Irish rovers and deposited in the cathedral of Christ Church in Dublin.

The precinct of the churchyard claims a far higher antiquity than the church. It is a square or 220 feet by 130. the sides are strong walls 17 feet high and 6 feet thick, the 4th side open to the precipitous rocks of the harbour. At each corner of the wall is an oval tower. The masonry of the whole is evidently Roman: the mortar very hard and mixed with much coarse pebble. Along the walls are 2 rows of round holes about 4 inches in diameter, which penetrate them. They are in all respects like those at Segontium and nicely plastered within.

The use of this port to the Romans in the passage from various places to the ports of Lancashire and that of Chester is very evident. They could not find a better place than this to run into in case of hard weather as it projected farthest into the Vergivian sea. If (as is very probable) they had commerce with Ireland, no place was better adapted. The Romans, it is true, never made a settlement in that country but they certainly traded with it even in the time of Agricola. I took a walk from the town to the top of The Head in search of other antiquities. On the Pen Caergybi, or the summit of the mountain, are foundations of a circular building strongly cemented with the same sort of mortar as the fort in the town. It seems to have been a Pharos, a necessary director in these seas.

From the top of this mountain I had a distinct view of the isle of Caergybi, it being at that time high-water and the channel filled on each side of Rhyd-Pont bridge. The isle is of unequal breadth and greatly indented. The part of the Head fronting the sea is either an immense precipice or hollowed into most magnificent caves. Birds of various kinds breed in the rocks; among them are peregrine falcons, shags, herons, razor-bills and guillemots. Their eggs are sought for food and are gotten by means of a man who is lowered down by a rope held by one or more persons. Within memory, the person let down by his weight overpowered the other and pulled him down so that both perished miserably.

Near the comfortable inn called the Gwyndy, in the middle of the island, is Bodychen, an ancient building once the seat of Rhys ap Llywelyn ap Hwlcyn, first sheriff of this country and a potent man in the time of Henry VIII. The founder went to Bosworth field to assist Henry VII with a company of foot. In return, he was sworn sheriff of Ynys Môn for life. He made his house (now converted into a barn) the county jail, the dungeon whereof is still to be seen. In the last century it passed to the Sparrows of Red Hill by the marriage of the heiress of this place.

On the right is the church of Llantrisant, remarkable for the monument of the Reverend Hugh Williams D.D., an ancestor of the Wynnstay family and father to Sir William Williams, speaker of the house of commons and solicitor general in 1687.

Before I leave the island, I beg leave to communicate a brief account of its population. By Paul Panton's remarks ('*Philosophical Transactions*' 63 Part 1 page 180), there were 2,010 households or families in Ynys Môn on August 13th 1563, allowing 5 to a family. In 1776 the number of houses was about 3,956 so the whole number of persons was 19,780 (again allowing 5 persons to a family), which wants only 340 to double the number of inhabitants in the intervening time.

Continue my journey from Porthaethwy Ferry up a steep road and soon descend into Bangor, a small town seated between 2 low hills in a valley opening to the bay of Biwmares. This is the episcopal seat. The prelate is very indifferently lodged in a palace near the cathedral which appears to have been rebuilt by Bishop Skeffington who died in 1533 at the abbey of Beaulieu where he had been abbot. He directed that his body should be interred there and his heart at Bangor before the image of the patron saint: St Deiniol.

About the year 550, Maelgwn Gwynedd, one of those gentry who, growing virtuous in old age, "made a sacrifice to God of the Devil's leavings" (Swift), converted the college into a bishopric and appointed Daniel to be the first bishop.

The cathedral was destroyed in the year 1071. It was afterwards rebuilt for we find that in 1212 King John invaded the country, forced the bishop, Robert of Shrewsbury, from before the altar, and obliged him to pay 200 hawks for his ransom. In 1402 it was reduced again to ruin by the rage of Glyndŵr and lay unrestored during 90 years. There is nothing remarkable within except a few tombs. That wise and valiant prince Owain Gwynedd lies beneath an arch, with a flowery cross cut on a flat stone. He died, regretted by his countrymen and feared by his foes, in 1169.

Hugh Lupus, in his barbarous inroad into Ynys Môn, founded a castle at Bangor in order to carry on his ravages with greater security. The site was pointed out to me by the reverend Mr E.R. Owen (a gentleman to whom this part of the work is under frequent obligations). It lies nearly a quarter of a mile eastward of the town, on the ridge of hills which bound the south-east side of the vale, and nearly the same distance from the port. The castle stood on a rocky and, in many parts, precipitous hill. Three sides of the walls are easily traced, extending 120 yards of the south-east side, 66 on the south-west, ending at a precipice, and 40 yards on the north-east, ending in the same manner. On the 4th side, the natural strength of the place rendered a farther defence useless. We know not the time of its demolition; it was probably suffered to fall into ruin as soon as the earl had effected his design.

On leaving Bangor, I took the road towards Conwy. At a small

*Bangor Cathedral*

distance from the former, crossed Abercegin, a small creek fordable at low water, from whence are annually imported many millions of slates. The quarries are about 5 miles distant, near the entrance into Nant Ffrancon, at a small distance from the river Ogwen. They are the property of Lord Penrhyn who has added greatly to the population of the country by the great improvements he has made in the slate business. The quarries are now the source of a prodigious commerce. When his lordship came to the estate, not 1,000 tons were exported, the country was scarcely passable, the roads not better than very bad horse paths, the cottages wretched and the farmers so poor as in all the tract not able to produce more than 3 miserable teams. At present a noble coach road is made, even beyond Nant Ffrancon, and the terrors of the Benglog quite done away. About 103 broad wheeled carts are in constant employ in carrying the slates down to the port: upwards of 12,000 tons in the year 1792 and it is expected that in a very short time the quantity will be increased to 16,000. The port is going to be enlarged; it is always filled with vessels: I saw one upwards of 300 tons burden. Such are the improvements in our flourishing kingdom that it is with difficulty the quarries can supply the demand. The slates are sent to Liverpool and up the Mersey by means of a canal to all the internal parts of the kingdom, and to Hull from whence numbers are shipped for Ireland, Flanders and even the West-Indies.

At the port his lordship has established a great manufacture of writing slates. Before that, we were entirely supplied from Switzerland: that trade is now ceased; the Swiss manufacturers are become bankrupt. The number of writing slates manufactured and exported from Port Penrhyn in the last 12 months is 136,000. The consumption of timber in this very trifling article is upwards of 3,000 feet in the year and the number of workmen employed from 25 to 30. I must recommend to the curious traveller a ride to the quarries. The whole neighbourhood is made by the houses and cottages of the quarriers, built after the elegant design of Mr Wyatt, and Ogwen bank is a beautiful lodge for the reception of Lord Penrhyn whenever he chooses to treat his friends with the sight of his laudable changes in the face of this once desolate country.

On the summit of a hill not very remote from Port Penrhyn, commanding a most charming view, stands Penrhyn, an ancient house once beautifully embosomed with venerable oaks. The house is said to have been built on the site of a palace of Rhodri Mawr, Prince of Wales, who began his reign in 720. It continued long in our princes. In 987 it was levelled to the ground by Maredudd ap Owain who, in that year, invaded North Wales and slew Cadwallon ap Ieuan, the reigning prince.

In the reign of Queen Elizabeth, Pyrs Gruffudd, lord of the place, distinguished himself as a naval officer. He sailed from Biwmares on April 20th 1588 and arrived at Plymouth on May 4th where he was most honourably received by that gallant commander Sir Francis Drake. He shared with the other men of rank and gallantry in the honour of defeating the Spanish Armada. After that distinguished victory, he joined with Sir Francis Drake and Sir Walter Raleigh in their different expeditions against the Spaniards in the West Indies but, in the reign of James I continuing his depredations against the Spaniards after peace was proclaimed, was called to account and obliged to mortgage his estate to defray the expenses. The house was rebuilt in the reign of Henry VI by Gwilym ap Gruffudd. Richard Pennant, now Lord Penrhyn, possesses the whole estate by virtue of his marriage with Anne Susannah, daughter and sole heiress of the late General Warburton of Winnington.

The bards were very liberal of their incense to the great men of this house, especially to Sir William Gruffudd, chamberlain of North Wales. Hywel ap Reinallt addressed to him a *cywydd* on his being imprisoned by Richard III along with Lord Strange for his attachment to the Earl of Richmond, afterwards Henry VII. And Lewis Môn thus addresses Sir Gruffudd on his leading a number of his countrymen to France in the following reign:

*Nid â dy fath, odid fydd,*
*I dir Gien dragywydd.*

Their equal (perhaps) will never go
To the land of Guienne.

From Penrhyn I visited the church of Llandegai, anciently called Corarian, about a mile distant from the house. It is finely situated on a lofty bank above the Ogwen and commands a beautiful view. It is a small and neat structure in the form of a cross with the tower in the centre supported within by 4 arches.

From Llandegai I descended and crossed the wooden bridge, now changed into a very handsome one of stone, over the furious torrent Ogwen which, a little lower, discharges itself into the sea at Aberogwen and near which is the ruin of the old chapel Capel Ogwen and certain entrenchments, defences of this part of the country. I soon quitted the great road to visit Carnedd Llywelyn and Carnedd Dafydd. In my way, near a field called Caer Gwilym Ddu, is an artificial cave in which (tradition says) was interred William de Breos, executed by Llywelyn the

Great on suspicion of too great familiarity with his royal consort. From hence I begin a steep ascent and leave on the left the vast mountain Moel Wnion and the strange serrated rocks Bera Mawr and Bera Bach. The Gyrn appeared on our right and Drosgl in front. On the right, farther on, projected into the bottom the lofty peaked Moel yr Elen (*Hill of the Fawn*), seeming like a buttress to Carnedd Llywelyn; and between it and Carnedd Dafydd lies the little vale of Cwm Pen-llafar, fertile in grass.

We proceeded on the sloping sides of the Drosgl and near Carnedd y Filiast and Carnedd y Lladron. Passing over Clogwyn yr Heliwr (*Rock of the Hunter*) and ascending the steep and stony side of Carnedd Llywelyn, reach the broad and flat summit and quickly decide its height to be far inferior to that of its rival Yr Wyddfa. The view is amazingly great. At some distance are Yr Wyddfa and its neighbouring alps. The Glyders, Tryfan and Carnedd y Filiast (*Rock of the Bitch Greyhound*) appear immediately beneath. The front of the last is an even slope of rock, smooth and uniform, and so slippery that if the fox, in extreme danger, takes over it in wet weather, it falls down and perishes.

In my return from this sublime ride, I called at Coed Mawr, seated in the midst of lofty trees every now and then opening so as to admit sight of the exalted mountains and rocks soaring above with misty tops. This had long been the residence of a family of the same name, and of later years, by the marriage of the heiress, the property of the Pughs of Penrhyn in Creuddyn.

Continue my ride towards the shore, towards Aber, a small village with a church, in the gift of Lord Bulkeley, seated at the mouth of a deep glen which runs straight a mile and a half between the mountains and bounded on one side by a magnificent rock called Maes y Gaer. At the extremity of this glen a mountain presents a concave front, in the centre of which a vast cataract precipitates down a double fall. The lowest is of a very great height and forms partly a broad white sheet, partly a snowy dew, not unlike the Staub-bauch (*dusty cascade*) in Switzerland.

At the entrance of the glen, close to the village, is a very large artificial mount, flat at the top and near 60 feet in diameter, widening towards the base. It was once the site of a castle belonging to Llywelyn the Great. Some foundations are yet to be seen round the summit and, in digging, traces of buildings have been discovered. In this place was detected the intrigue of William de Breos with the wife of Llywelyn. It seems that William, by chance of war, had fallen into the hands of our prince at which time probably the familiarity with the princess commenced but was not discovered till after he was released on a large ransom. In the following year (1229). Llywelyn inveigled Breos into his power by an invitation to celebrate the feast of Easter. After an elegant banquet, the prince reproached him with his crime and caused him to be dragged from his presence and hung on an adjacent hill.

I continued my journey from Aber along the rich recess, enjoying a fine view of the entrance into the Menai with its wooded shores of Ynys Môn and Ynys Seiriol, and the great expanse of water between them and Llandudno or Pen-y-Gogarth, the vast cape rising like the rock of Gibraltar high out of the waves. Before me soared the great promontory of Penmaen-mawr, protruding itself into the sea. A little farther is the small village and church of Llanfairfechan from whence is a very short ride to the once tremendous road over this celebrated rock.

In past times it was justly the terror of the traveller; extremely narrow, bad and stony, the danger increasing by reason of the precipice gaining additional height. Generally it was without the protection of a wall to secure him in case of a false step which might in the loftiest place precipitate him some scores of yards either on sharp rocks or into the sea, according to the state of the tide. A vein of crumbling stratum in one part so contracted the road as to excite new horrors. The parliament in London eased the fears of the travellers by a generous aid which, by means of the judicious employment of John Sylvester about the year 1772, effected what was before thought beyond the reach of art to remedy. The road is now widened to a proper breadth and, near the verge of the precipice, secured by a strong wall. The descent towards Penmaen-bach which before was hardly practicable, is now destroyed and the road is brought on a level for 2 or 3 miles at a vast height above a return of rich slopes and the deep bottom of Dwygyfylchi till we arrive at the rude back of that promontory when we labour up the steep ascent of Sychnant. From the top of Sychnant, the road is continued about two miles on a perpetual descent to the town of Conwy.

The breach occasioned by the crumbling stratum is now effectually repaired by a series of arches, the just admiration of travellers and a high credit to the ingenious contriver. One danger yet remains which must for ever baffle the art of man: the side of this great rock above the road breaks into millions of vast masses, depending often on precarious tenures which, loosened by frequent torrents, sometimes (though rarely) descend in stony streams.

Two or three accidents which have happened on this road will remain as miracles. An exciseman fell from the highest part and escaped unhurt. The reverend Mr Jones, who in 1762 was rector of Llaneilian in Ynys Môn, fell with his horse, and a midwife behind him, down the steepest part. The midwife perished, as did the nag. The divine, with great philosophy, unsaddled the steed and marched off with the trappings, exulting at his preservation.

Above a century ago, Siôn Humphries of Llanfairfechan had made his addresses to Anne Thomas of Creuddyn on the other side of the Conwy river. They had made an appointment to meet at a fair in the town of Conwy. He in his way fell over Penmaen Mawr; she was overset in the ferry-boat and was the only person saved out of more than 80. They were married and lived very long together in the parish of Llanfair. She was buried April 11th 1744 aged 116. He survived her 5 years and was buried December 10th 1749 in the parish churchyard where their graves are familiarly shown to this day.

I have more than once visited the summit of this noted rock to view the fortifications. The ascent is laborious. A Mr Caswell, at the request of John Flamsteed the great astronomer, measured the height and found it to be from the sands 1,545 feet.

After climbing for some space among the loose stones, the front of three if not four walls presented themselves very distinctly one above the other. In most places the facings appeared very perfect but all of dry work. I measured the height of one wall which was at that time 9 feet, the thickness 7 feet and a half. Between these walls were innumerable small buildings, mostly circular and regularly faced within and without but not disposed in any certain order. These had been much higher as is evident from the fall of stones which lie scattered at their bottoms. Their diameter in general is from 12 to 18 feet but some were far less, not exceeding 5 feet. A well cut in the live rock is always filled with water supplied by the rains and kept full by the frequent impending vapours.

This strong-hold of the Celts is exactly of the same kind with those on Garn Fadryn, Garn Boduan and Tre'r Ceiri. The white beam (Aria Theophrasti) is frequent on the sides of this rock and in many similar places in Wales. No use is made of it in our country. The Swiss procure from the berries a good spirit. The wood is very hard and excellent for flutes; it was also esteemed to make the best charcoal.

I descended from the summit into a hollow between the Penmaen and an adjacent mountain. Got upon my horse and directed my course on a good sheep-walk towards Conwy. For a considerable length of the way I saw circles of stones of various diameters and great Carneddau.

*Part of the interior of Conwy Castle*

# Chapter Twelve

# Conwy to Abergele

ENTERED CONWY at the upper gate. A more ragged town is scarcely to be seen within, or a more beautiful one without. The situation is on a steep slope to the verge of the river, here a mile broad at high water. The form is nearly triangular, surrounded with lofty walls guarded by 24 round towers. A castle of matchless magnificence rises on a lofty rock at one corner.

In front is an extensive quay from which is a delightful view up and down the river. The opposite side is hilly, varied with woods and gentlemen's seats, and the bifurcated hill of Deganwy, a fortress. The ground called Arcadia, laid out by my worthy friend and old school-fellow Owen Holland, and Plas Tirion, the house of the reverend Mr Owen Jones, well merit a visit from the traveller.

The castle was built by Edward I in the year 1284 who, I believe, employed the architect who built Caernarfon. One side is bounded by the river; another by a creek full of water at every tide and most beautifully shaded by hanging woods. The great hall suited the magnificence of the founder. It is of a curved form, conformable to the bend of the outward walls, including one end with a large window which seems to have been the private chapel. It extended 130 feet in length, was 32 broad and of a fine height.

The town contains but few inhabitants, a considerable space being vacant of buildings. It has 4 entrances: the upper gate; the lower, next to the water; a portal between that and the castle; and another to the creek called Porth y Felin or the gate to the mill.

The ferry is at present the property of the owner of Marle. An order was issued by Edward II for either repairing the boat or building a new one, for the use of which the inhabitants were to pay 8 marks. At low-water the river is not 50 yards broad nor above 8 feet deep. The spring-tides rise 12 feet but the approach to this port is unsafe by reason of sand-banks.

There are some remains of the Cistercian abbey founded in 1185 by Llywelyn ap Iorwerth, Prince of North Wales, in honour of the Blessed Virgin and All Saints. A long vaulted room of good masonry, worked with clay but plastered with lime, and a Saxon door are still to be seen. He endowed it with lands to a vast extent in Gwynedd and Ynys Môn and with privileges of great value. It was exempted not only from the maintenance of all men, horses, dogs and hawks but even those of the prince. No one was to interfere in the elections or affairs of the house. They were to enjoy all benefits of wrecks on the shores of their property in the same manner as the prince did on his but no advantage was to be taken of similar misfortunes to the religious men; all their goods so wrecked were to be restored. They and their servants were to be exempt in all parts from tolls, pontage and the like, and their free passage over the Menai, Conwy, Abermaw and Dyfi is particularly provided for.

Conwy was a place of note before the English conquest. It probably had some sort of fortress before the existence of the present, its ancient name being Caer Gyffin, Gyffin being that of the stream that flows into the creek beneath the castle. Camden tells us that Hugh Lupus had fortified the place, I suppose on his march into Ynys Môn in 1098.

Among the illustrious persons buried in the church was Cynan ap Owain Gwynedd who was interred in the year 1200 in a monk's cowl because, says Powel (*History of Wales*, 252) "it was then made to believe by the monks and friars that that strange weed was a sure defence betwixt their souls and hell, howsoever they died". A very rude figure, cut on stone, preserves the memory of Mary, mother to Archbishop Williams, who died of child-birth of twins October 10th 1585. A singular epitaph on a Mr Hookes proves the remarkable fecundity of the family: Here lyeth the body of Nicholas Hookes of Conwy, Gent. who was the 41st child of his father William Hookes, Esq; by Alice his wife, and the father of 27 children; who died the 20th day of March 1637.

The town was almost depopulated by the plague in 1607 and numbers of people were buried in the streets. It was observed to break out here within weeks of the time it appeared in London, probably brought here by some fugitives.

Several years ago, the folly of some of the inhabitants, by getting stones from the rock beneath one of the great towers, brought down a vast segment. The ruins are the most awful I ever beheld, lying in stupendous fragments on the shore, some so unbroken as to preserve both the grand external rotundity and the internal concavity: a hardened cement of stone and mortar 11 feet thick.

From Conwy I took the road towards Caerhun, the Canovium of the Romans. In my way passed near Cymryd, a place noted for a bloody battle in 880 between Anarawd, Prince of Wales, and the Saxons under Edred, duke of Mercia. The Welsh were victorious and drove the invaders back into their own country. Anarawd styled the battle Dial Rhodri (*Rhodri's Revenge*), for his father Rhodri Mawr had the year before been slain by the Saxons.

Passed by the ferry of Tal-y-cafn. At a small distance is a large artificial mount called Bryn y Castell, probably the site of a watchtower belonging to Canovium. Caer Rhun, the old Canovium, lay in a low spot near the river. There are still be seen the remains of Roman bricks and a sunk building divided into 2 parts, probably the remains of a hypocaust.

I continued my journey through the wooded parish of Llansanffraid Glan Conwy, beautifully sloping to the water's edge. The route I took was towards Llandudno, the grand boundary of the entrance of the Conwy. From the road, in many parts, are the most august views of the vast expanse of the river and the majestic towers of Conwy. Similar views, and old fortified towns, I have seen on the Rhine, but in magnificence far inferior to these. After a ride of about three miles, descend to a flat. Pass by Marle, a house of fine appearance but now little more than a case, having suffered by fire about 40 years ago.

High above Marle is Bodysgallen, the property of Sir Roger Mostyn in right of his wife Margaret, daughter of the reverend Hugh Wynne. I find Richard Mostyn in possession of it. It is a place of great antiquity as appears by the ruins of a small castelet, now hid in woods, on the top of a small hill near the present house. Bodysgallen signifies the dwelling place of Scallan, in all probability a word corrupted from Caswallon, the owner in some distant period. It was one of those townships called Tre Welyog, not entirely free. The tenants were originally possessors of hereditary estates which were divided and subdivided among their posterity to the 4th descent, after which they became possessed by branches independent of each other, all of whom paid for their own land.

From hence is a small walk to Gloddaeth, a seat of Sir Roger Mostyn's, placed on the slope of a very extensive hill or limestone rock clothed with successful plantations by Sir Roger, grandfather of the preset possessor. Every flight of path presents new and grand objects: the great windings of the river towards Llanrwst, the lofty towers of Conwy, and beyond a long extent of alps with Moel Siabod, Drum, Carnedd Llywelyn and Carnedd Dafydd appearing with distinguished height. From a little higher ascent is opened to us the discharge of the Conwy into the sea, sublimely bounded by the immense Orme's Head of Llandudno, the vast promontory of Penmaen-mawr, the Ynys Seiriol and the long extent of Ynys Môn.

Eglwys Rhos, the parish church, is celebrated for the death of the prince Maelgwn Gwynedd who had taken shelter here to avoid the *Fâd Felen* or yellow pestilence which at that time raged through Europe. The Britons, like the Romans, personified disease. In this instance it was to assume either the form of a basilisk, or the powers of one, under the form of a fair women who slew Maelgwn with a glance as he incautiously looked out of the window.

The small remains of Degannwy are on 2 small hills near the shore of the Conwy. The walls crossed the space between the hills and ran up their sides. On the summit of one is the vestige of a round tower and here and there are a few foundations of walls on the accessible parts. I cannot discover the founder of the fortress on whose ruins I contemplate. It might have been Robert of Rhuddlan. We are told this country was parcel of the possessions of the earls of Chester and that Robert was in it when he came to his fate. On July 3rd 1088 our brave prince Gruffudd ap Cynan, with 3 ships, entered the Conwy and, landing under the castle at high water, left the ships on shore at the recess of the tide. He ravaged the neighbouring country and drove towards his vessels a great booty of men and cattle. Robert, indignant at this, descended from his fortress attended by a single soldier, Osbern de Orgar, and without any defensive armour except his shield. The Welsh attacked him with missile weapons and, filling his shield so full of darts that it feel under their weight, the enemy rushed on him, cut off his head and, fastening it to the mast, sailed off in savage triumph. Llywelyn Fawr destroyed this castle but it was rebuilt in 1210 by Randle Blondevil, Earl of Chester. King John lay for some time encamped under its walls in the year 1211 and was reduced to severe difficulty by the policy of Llywelyn who came between him and England and cut off his resources. Henry III fared even worse on the same spot in 1245. Degannwy was totally dismantled in 1260 by our last prince Llywelyn ap Gruffudd.

Not far from hence, on the top of a low hill near Bryniau, is an ancient tower. Its form is circular, its height about 20 feet, the diameter 12. Its walls compose only two thirds of a circle; the rest is open to the top. The finishing of the walls is complete, without any appearance of there ever having been a door, and this opening is to the land. Within are the marks of 2 floors. Round the inside are 3 rows of square holes, none of which pass through the building. Its walls are of great thickness and the mortar appears very ancient. I can make no conjecture about the use but describe it in order to exercise the talents of others.

Continued my ride along the shore by the flat isthmus which connects the high land of Gloddaith with the great promontory Llandudno. Ride along part of the last on a narrow road above the sea, having on the right steep hills and precipices. From Gogarth, I ascended on a long and steep path to the top of Llandudno, a beautiful sheepwalk consisting of a fine turf, except where the rock appears, extending near 4 miles in length and 1 in breadth. The western extremity is a vast precipice, the haunt of various sea-fowls in the season of breeding. The gulls possess the lowest part; above them the razor-bills and guillemots have their quarters; over them croak the cormorants. Herons occupy the highest regions and scattered in different parts are a few puffins and black guillemots. The peregrine falcon builds on these rocks. The kind was in the days of falconry so excellent that the great minister Burleigh sent a letter of thanks to an ancestor of Sir Roger Mostyn for a present of a cast of hawks from this place.

Falconry was held in high esteem among the Welsh. Our prince had his chief falconer who held 4th rank among the officials of his court. He held his lands free and had a double portion of provender for his horse. The prince supplied him with woollen clothes, the princess with linen. He brought his cup with him into the hall but was not allowed to drink more than would quench his thirst lest he should get fuddled and neglect his hawks.

From Rhos Fynach the land recedes inwards and forms a pretty bay. Penmaen Rhos, a great limestone rock, juts into the sea at the end of the bay. In my memory the traveller went along a narrow path cut on its front, like the road on Penmaen-mawr but infinitely more terrible and dangerous. A fine coach-road has lately been formed far behind this precipice. From thence I descended to Llanddulas, a small village and church. In one of the deep bottoms of this neighbourhood was betrayed the unfortunate prince Richard II who had been deceived by the Earl of Northumberland to go along with him to Conwy to meet Bolingbroke and settle amicably the quarrel between them. Hereabouts he suddenly found himself surrounded by a large band of armed men placed there by the treacherous earl who, seizing on Richard, delivered him captive to the usurper in Y Fflint castle.

A little farther on the right hand, high above the road, is Cefn yr Ogof, a lofty precipice, white unless where darkened by the ivy which spreads along the front. In the middle is the most magnificent entrance into a cave which Britain can boast. It seems like the portal of a noble cathedral, arched, and divided within by what has the appearance of a great column.

Abergele is bounded to the right by high lime-stone hills, at times productive of lead ore. On one of them, called Copa yr Wylfa (*the mount of the watchtower*) and projecting from the rest, is a very strong British post. In a glen beneath is a ditch called Ffos y Bleiddiaid (*the ditch of the Wolves*), possibly from the frequency of those animals in these parts.

From Abergele I ascended to the neighbouring parish of Cegidog. High above this place, on the top of a hill called Pen y Parc, is a very strong post said to have been occupied by Owain Gwynedd after his fine retreat before Henry II whom he kept here at bay and politically secured his dominions from further invasion.

## Chapter Thirteen

# From Downing to Trefaldwyn, 1776

ON WEDNESDAY July 4th 1776 I left home, breakfasted with the reverend Mr Lloyd at Caerwys, and with him descended into the pretty little vale which leads from Yr Wyddgrug to Denbigh. At Llys Coed y Mynydd lived Ednowain Bendew (*Ednowain the Strong-headed*), Lord of Tegengl in 1079 and one of the 15 tribes of North Wales. These llwythau or tribes were the nobility of North Wales. They were, at different times, lords of distinct districts and called to that honour by several princes. The latest were about the time of Dafydd ap Owain Gwynedd who began his reign in 1169.

After resting one night at Corwen, proceed as far as Llandrillo on the road to Bala. Near that village turn left into a narrow glen, much wooded, watered by a rude torrent and bounded by high hills. At its extremity, begin to ascend Milltir Gerrig (*the Stony Mile*), a bwlch or pass amidst the Berwyn hills, about a mile in length with the mountains soaring on each side to a stupendous height. It is the great pass in these parts from Meirionnydd into Trefaldwyn and divides the counties. The latter is called by the Welsh Sir Drefaldwyn (the shire of the town of Baldwin, lieutenant of the marches in the time of the Conqueror). The name of the town was later changed to Montgomery, derived from Roger de Montgomery, the founder of the castle.

The descent from this pass is very steep but a fine road was then forming with the great view of giving the Irish a shorter way into their country through Oswestry. This is one of the vast designs of the present age which will effect communications with places before almost inaccessible.

On arriving at the bottom, I again found myself in narrow vales, loftily bounded. After about 3 miles riding reached Llangynog, a small village in the diocese of St Asaph. This place was the source of short-lived wealth to the maternal relation of the present Earl of Powys. A lead mine was discovered here in the year 1692 which was in most parts a vein of 3 yards and a half thick and was worked to a depth of 100 yards, when the water became too powerful. It continued in a flourishing state near 40 years, yielded about 4,000 tons annually, was sold at 7 pounds a ton and smelted on the spot, bringing the family a clear revenue of 20,000 pounds a year.

A slate quarry has been discovered of late years in the parish. About 904,000 were sold from November 1st 1775 to November 1st 1776 which sell at the rate of from 6 to 20 shillings a thousand, but the want of water carriage is a great loss to the work.

About 2 miles distance from Llangynog I turned up a small valley to the right to pay my devotions to the shrine of St Monacella or, as the Welsh style her, Melangell. Her legend relates that she was the daughter of an Irish monarch who had determined to marry her to a nobleman of his court. The princess had vowed celibacy. She fled from her father's dominions and took refuge in this place where she lived for 15 years without seeing the face of man. Brochwel Ysgythrog, Prince of Powys, being one day a hare-hunting, was amazed to find a virgin of surprising beauty engaged in deep devotion with the hare he had been pursuing under her robe, boldly facing the dogs. These retired to a distance, howling, notwithstanding all the efforts of the sportsmen to make them seize their prey. Brochwel heard her story and gave to God and her a parcel of lands to be a sanctuary to all that fled there. He desired her to found an abbey on the spot. She did so and died abbess in a good old age. She was buried in the neighbouring church, called Pennant and from her distinguished by the addition of Melangell.

In the churchyard is a stone with the figure of an armed man which now serves as a common grave stone but once covered the remains of the eldest son of Owain Gwynedd, Iorwerth Drwyndwn (*Edward with the broken nose*), who was put aside of the succession on account of the blemish. Hither he had fled from the cruelty of his brother Dafydd ap Owain Gwynedd, this place having been one of our most celebrated sanctuaries. Tradition says he was killed not far from hence at a place called Bwlch Croes Iorwerth.

This valley is exceedingly picturesque, inclosed by hills on all sides except its entrance; watered by the Tanat which springs not far off. The upper end is bounded by 2 vast precipices down which, at times, fall 2 great cataracts. Between them juts out the great and rude promontory of Moel Ddu.

I made an excursion to Llwydiarth, a large old house in the parish of

Llanwddyn seated in a hilly naked country. It was formerly the property of the great family of the Vaughans, descended from Aleth Hen King of Dyfed. The estate was conveyed to the late Sir Watkin Williams Wynn by his first wife, daughter and heiress to the last owner. From one part of the ride had a view into Ceredigion and of the great naked mountain of Pumlumon, covered with heath or moory grass.

Dr William Morgan, who first translated the Bible into Welsh, was vicar of St Dogfan's church in Llanrhaeadr-ym-Mochnant. He was rewarded by Queen Elizabeth with the bishopric of Llandaf in 1595 and was removed to that of St Asaph in 1601 where he died September 10th 1604 and was interred in the cathedral. The facetious but learned preacher Dr South was the last rector of the parish. On his decease, the rectorial tithes were appropriated by act of parliament to the maintenance of the choir and repair of the cathedral church of St Asaph.

The abundance of sheep which enliven these hills brought great wealth at the time I visited. The flannel manufacturer, and that of a coarse cloth for the army and for covering the poor negroes in the West Indies, is manufactured in most parts of the county. It is sent and sold rough to Shrewsbury, a practice very contrary to the interest of the locality.

Ride for some time on the Oswestry road. Ascend to the right; go near Bryn Gwyn, a seat of William Mostyn, above which is a circular Brythonic post. Numbers of them front the low country on the hills which jut into it, as if guards to protect the internal parts from invasion. Across the road in one place I met the vestiges of a very strong rampart to defend a pass into the vale of Meifod which soon after appeared in view. The church and village are situated in the middle of the valley, which is quite flat, extending more than 5 miles in length and half a mile broad. The church is dedicated to St Tysilio, a prince of Powys, the supporter of the British churches against Austin the Monk.

Not far above Meifod is a union of 2 rivers, both named Efyrnwy. Both of them diverge considerably from each other and take their rise remote from one another. On a steep bank above one of the rivers stood Mathrafal, once the seat of the princes of Powys, the name at present preserved by a farm-house. I could easily trace the site of the ancient castle; it occupied the space of about 2 acres. One side was guarded by the steep over the river, the other 3 sides by a vast rampart of stone and earth and a very deep foss. A high exploratory mount fills one corner from which is a clear view of all that passes up and down the vale. The castle was possessed by Robert de Vepont, a baron high in favour with King John. In 1112, Llywelyn ap Iorwerth laid siege to it but the king

161

coming with a potent army obliged Llywelyn to retire and after that caused the castle to be demolished.

A few miles farther, rode through the village of Castell Caereinion which is seated near the Efyrnwy. A castle was built here in 1155 by Madog ap Maredudd, Prince of Powys. I had not the leisure to enquire whether there were any remains. The country for 7 miles more continued hilly and full of unpleasant commons. Reach Gregynog, the seat of Arthur Blainey whose hospitality I experienced for 2 or 3 days. Under his conduct I saw every thing in the neighbourhood which merited attention. The very worthy owner is descended from Brochwel Ysgythrog. The elder branch of the family has been ennobled in Ireland since the year 1620 by the title of Lord Blainey of Monaghan, an honour well earned by Sir Edward Blainey for services in Ireland in the reigns of Queen Elizabeth and her successor.

One evening I was conducted to Castell Dolforwyn, a castle on the high ridge of a hill, very steep and almost surrounded by a wooded dingle. At the bottom runs a small brook which falls into the Severn about a mile distant.

It is the misfortune of this part of the country to be destitute of several most necessary materials. The rich are obliged to burn wood instead of coal, and the poor a wretched turf. The moral of this is: Plant and Preserve Your Woods! Lime is extremely remote and stone fit for masonry at a vast distance. From the head of the Severn as low as Llandrinio, there is not a stone bridge. At times, one part of the country becomes inaccessible to the other for want of bridges.

The following day our ride was directed towards Caersws, a place of Roman antiquity. Our way lay over some high grassy lands. On Gwynfynydd was easily traced the Roman road called Sarn Swsan. It runs from Caersws, points towards Meifod and is distinctly traced as far as the banks of Llyn Efyrnwy near Llyffin. I am not able to pursue it either to or from Meifod but the late Dr Worthington assured me that it was met with in his parish at Street Fawr, near Coed y Clawdd and from Pen y Street to Caerfach which is supposed to have been a small Roman camp.

The mountains of Carno, like the mountains of Gilboa, were celebrated for the fall of the mighty. The fiercest battle in our annals happened in 1077 amidst these hills when Gruffudd ap Cynan, supported by Rhys ap Tudur Prince of southern Wales, disputed the sovereignty of North Wales with Trahaearn ap Caradog the reigning prince. After a most bloody contest, victory declared itself in favour of the first; Trahaearn and his kinsmen, disdaining flight, fell on the spot. Gruffudd ap Cynan was put into possession of his rightful throne which he filled during 57 years with great dignity.

The church of Carno belonged to the knights of St John of Jerusalem who are said to have had a house near it. As one part of their business was the protection of their fellow creatures from violence, it is very possible that they might have had a station in these parts which were long filled with a lawless banditti.

Opposite to Llandinam, on the summit of a high mountain, is a Celtic post called Y Gaer Fechan or the Little Fortress, surrounded with a number of fosses, from one to 5 according as the strength or weakness of the parts required.

Llanidloes is a small town with a great market for yarn which is manufactured here into fine flannels and sent weekly by waggon-loads to Y Trallwng. The church is dedicated to St Idloes. Within are 6 arches, the columns surrounded with neat round pillars ending in capitals of palm-leaves. The inhabitants assert that they were brought from the abbey of Cwm-hir in Maesyfed. A date on the roof is 1542 which soon followed the period of monastic ruin in this kingdom.

This is a country of sheepwalks. The flocks, like those of Spain, are driven to them from distant parts to feed on the summer herbage. The farms in the valleys are only appendages, for winter habitations and provisions. A coarse slate is found in the neighbouring hills but there still remains in many parts the ancient covering of the country, shingles, heart of oak split and cut into the form of slates. This was introduced by the Saxons as the word is derived from schindel which signifies the same thing.

A little beyond Llanidloes the vale closes. The Severn here dwindles into an inconsiderable stream. By wonderful instinct, salmon force their way from the ocean, higher up even than this distant spot, for the sake of depositing their spawn. The other fish are trouts, samlets, graylings and pike. The river runs in a hollow to its source 15 miles distant in the vast hill of Pumlumon. I was dissuaded from making it a visit, being informed that it was an uninteresting object: the base most extensive, the top boggy and the view over a dreary and almost uninhabited country. It gives rise to the Rheidol which flows to the sea near Aberystwyth, and the Wye which, precipitating from its fountains down some most romantic rocks, continues its course till it falls into the Severn below Cas-gwent.

After a most pleasing ride, return to Gregynog with my good host, the best shower of a country I ever had the good fortune of meeting.

On the morning I took leave of Gregynog and, attended by Mr Blainey, skirted the hilly country. Near the house of Nantcribba, the seat of Lord Viscount Hereford, rises a great conoid rock. A few years ago, on taking away the top, were discovered the remains of a little fort. On paring away the rubbish, it appeared to have been square with a round tower probably at each corner. One is tolerably entire and is only 9 feet diameter within; the wall 7 feet 7 inches thick. The place was probably ruined by fire for I observed some melted lead mixed with charcoal and several pieces of vitrified stuff. There is no history relative to it. Offa's ditch lies about 200 yards from the rock.

Enter a part of Shropshire at Walcot and, keeping southerly, soon reach Chirbury, a church and village which gave name to the hundred and title to the celebrated flower of chivalry Edward Lord Herbert in whom madness and abilities kept equal pace. Two miles farther is the neat small town of Trefaldwyn, partly built on the slope and partly on the summit of a hill beneath the shadow of one much higher. It owes its foundation to Baldwyn, lieutenant of the marches to William the Conqueror, from whom the Welsh called it Trefaldwyn. Roger de Montgomery fortified the place and called it after his own name. In 1094 the Welsh took the castle, put the garrison to the sword and carried destruction through the neighbouring parts. The king, William Rufus, assembled a vast army and repossessed himself of the low parts of the country. The Earl of Shrewsbury rebuilt the castle which the Welsh had destroyed. It was again ruined but we are not informed of the period, only that Henry III built a new castle there in 1221. Henry granted it to his great justiciary Hubert de Burgh with 200 marks annually and a greater salary in case of war. During the time it was possessed by Hubert it was besieged by the Welsh but speedily relieved by the English. In 1231, Llywelyn assembled a great army and so terrified Hubert that he evacuated the castle, which was seized and burnt by the exasperated prince.

In the civil wars it was seized for the use of parliament by Sir Thomas Middleton, in 1644. On the appearance of the king's army, he was obliged to make a sudden retreat to Oswestry and leave it ill provided with garrison and provisions. The royal forces under Lord Byron laid siege to it but Sir Thomas returned with Sir William Brereton, Sir John Meldrum and Sir William Fairfax, under the command of Brereton, with about 3,000 men, to the relief of the place. The king's army, 5,000 strong, took possession of the hill above the castle as the enemy approached. The castle was relieved and a most bloody battle ensued. The king's army descended from their post and at first gained considerable advantage but the forces of parliament, actuated by despair, made the most violent efforts and at length obtained complete victory.

The pursuit was continued near 20 miles. Above 500 were slain and 1,400 taken prisoner, The loss on the side of parliament was only 40 slain and about 60 wounded. The castle met with the fate of all others, being dismantled by order of the commons. The remains impend over the town on a projecting ridge of great height and steepness.

On a hill not far from the castle is a stupendous Celtic post. The approach is guarded by 4 great ditches with 2 or 3 entrances towards the main work. Two or 3 fosses run across the hill, the end of which is sufficiently guarded by the steepness. From the summit is a fine view of the vale of Trefaldwyn bounded by the hills of Shropshire.

The town was once defended by walls, strengthened by towers. It had also 4 gates: Chirbury, Arthur's, Ceri and Cedewen gate. There was a grant of Edward I to Bogo de Knouill, constable of the castle, giving him leave to fell certain wood on Corndon forest for repairing the walls and fosses round the town and castle, and another for the same purpose from Edward III permitting a toll for 7 years on several articles which were brought there to be sold: among others are enumerated squirrel skins.

Whether in old times this town abounded more than is usual with ladies of free lives and conversation I do not pretend to say; but very early the free burgesses had the privileges of the gogingstoole, cuckingstool or cokestoll, or what the Saxons called the scealfing-stole, therein to be placed with naked feet and dishevelled hair as an example to all beholders. Probably this was not found to answer the end intended; immersion, or ducking, was in after times added as an improvement and to effect a radical cure.

*Powys Castle*

## Chapter Fourteen

# Trefaldwyn to Shrewsbury

LEAVING TREFALDWYN, I took for 4 or 5 miles nearly the same road as I did in coming to it. Passed under Cefn Digoll. On this mountain may be said to have expired the liberties of Wales for here was the last contest against the power of our conqueror. After the death of Llywelyn, the northern Welshmen set up Madog, cousin to our slain prince. He assembled a great army and, after several eminent victories at Caernarfon, near Denbigh, Knockin, and again on the marches, was here overthrown in 1294 by the collected power of the lord marchers after a well-fought and long-contended engagement.

I must add that on this mountain Henry VII mustered the friends who promised to join him from northern Wales and Shropshire, and did not find one who had failed of his appointment. On which account the Welsh call it Digoll (*Without Loss*); the English name it the Long Mountain.

Cross the Severn near Llanlafryn, the seat of Price Jones. Soon after gaining this side of the river, I turned a little out of the road to Y Castell Coch, the seat of the Earl of Powys, placed on the ridge of a rock, having scarcely any area. You enter between 2 rounders; there are also the remains of round towers in other parts. Near the castle is a long gallery 117 feet by 20. It was once 167 feet but an apartment has been taken out of one end. This is of later date than the other building and was detached from it by a fire about 50 years ago. In the parlour, within the dwelling house, is a full-length of Roger Palmer, Earl of Castlemain, who owed his peerage to his wife, a royal mistress and afterwards duchess of Cleveland. James II sent him on an embassy to the pope to reconcile the church to these kingdoms of the holy see after their long lapse into heresy. The politic pope saw the folly of the design and never received the ambassador without being seized with a most seasonable fit of coughing which always

167

interrupted the subject of his errand. At length, wearied with the delay, he was advised to take petulance and threaten to leave Rome. His holiness, with great sang froid, affectionately recommended him to travel early in the morning and to rest at noon least he should endanger his health, and so ended this ridiculous business.

The first notice I find of this place is about the year 1110 when the renowned Welshman Cadwgan ap Bleddyn ap Cynfyn sought here an asylum from the persecution of his kindred and began a castle. While he was intent on the business, his nephew Madog came on him unawares and slew him. The building was continued, perhaps by Gwenwynwyn, for in 1191 it was besieged by Hubert archbishop of Canterbury. In 1233 Llywelyn ap Iorwerth overthrew this fortress which now assumed the name of Castell Coch (*Red Castle*) from the colour of the stones. His grandson Owain ap Gruffudd ap Gwenwynwyn remained in possession of the place. He left a daughter called Hawys Gadarn (*Hawys the Hardy*). Four of her uncles disputed her title to her father's land. Hawys wisely made a friend of Edward II who married her to John de Charlton, born near Wellington in Shropshire, and it continued in their posterity several generations.

Y Trallwng, a good town, is seated in the bottom not far from the castle. Great quantities of flannel, brought from the upper country, are sent from hence to Shrewsbury. The Severn begins to be navigable at the Poole stake about three quarters of a mile from the town.

Almost opposite to Y Trallwng, on the other side of the Severn, is Buttington (the Butdigingtune of the Saxons) where the Danes under Hesten took up their station in 894 after traversing great part of England. The generals of King Alfred instantly blocked them up so closely that the pagans were obliged to eat their horses for want of subsistence. At length, actuated by despair and famine, they attempted to force their way through the Saxon army and were defeated with such slaughter that a very few escaped to their own country.

The country from Poole towards Llanymynech is most beautifully broken into gentle risings, prettily wooded. Go by the small church of Llandysilio and soon after ford the Afon Efyrnwy, deviating a little from my intended route along the banks of the Severn to visit the public-spirited Mr Evans of Llwyn-y-groes who, in a most disinterested manner at his own hazard, is undertaking a beautiful map of North Wales. Continue at his house till morning and, in his company, visit Llanymynech. The church and village stand in a pretty situation on a bank above the Efyrnwy and very advantageous for trade. It lies at the opening of 3 valleys, at the intersection of 2 great public roads, and on a river navigable into the Severn some months of the year for barges of 50 tons. Great quantities of slates are sent from hence to Bristol and, of late years, up the Stourport canal to Birmingham and other places.

Ascend Llanymynech hill, a vast rock with the surface covered by a verdant turf beneath which is a verdant marble beautifully veined with red, streaked with white and capable of a good polish. This is the limestone of the place. The quantity burnt on this hill is inconceivable and the increase is 10 times greater since the improvement of the Trefaldwyn roads; it is carried even for manure 30 miles into that country. The season of carriage begins in March and ends in October. Copper, lead and calamine have been found of late years but there are undeniable proofs of working by the Romans. In a great artificial cave formed into several meanders in search of ores have been discovered Roman coins, among them an Antonius and a Faustina. Near the coins were found the skeleton of a man at full length; on his left arm a bracelet and by his side a battle-axe.

Not far from hence stood the castle of Carreg Hofa, a place of which I know nothing more than that it had been taken and pillaged in 1162 by Owain Cyfeiliog and Owain ap Madog ap Maredudd. It was soon restored for, in the year 1187, the latter was slain here in the night by Gwenwynwyn and Cadwallon, the sons of his former colleague.

From Llanymynech I rode to the New Bridge, a bridge of 7 arches over the Efyrnwy about 3 miles above the ford. This river is confined by a dam for the sake of the mill and forms a fine reach. The overflowing makes a pretty cascade and the views upwards, of small valleys and hanging woods, are exceedingly beautiful.

The river merits the title Piscosus Amnis as much as any I know. The number of fish which inhabit it animate the waters and add greatly to its beauty. Ausonius does not neglect that remark in his elegant poem on the Mosel:

'Intentos tamen usque oculos errore fatigant
Interludentes examina lubrica pisces'

I have not examined whether the Mosel affords more than is contained in the following list:

| FISH | WHEN IN SEASON |
| --- | --- |
| Salmon | Christmas to July |
| Trout Maredudd | March to September |
| Samlet Maredudd | ditto |
| Grayling | March to November |

| | |
|---|---|
| Minnow Maredudd | April to September |
| Perch | May to the end of September |
| Rough, or Pope | April to September |
| Carp | April to July |
| Tench, Roach | April to September |
| Dace Maredudd | ditto |
| Gudgeon | ditto |
| Bleak | June, July, August |
| Chub Maredudd | April to June |
| Loche Maredudd | March to September |
| Bullhead (or Miller's Thumb) | April to September |
| Shad | March and April |
| Eel Maredudd | June, July, August |
| Lamprey, Flounder | May to September |

Of these, only the species marked Maredudd frequent the Tanat, which falls into the Efyrnwy near the spot where this enumeration was made, such preference do fish give to certain waters.

After crossing the Severn, my road lay at the foot of that great mass of rocky mountains distinguished by the names of Breiddin, Moel y Golfa and Cefn y Castell. Their bases are prettily skirted with woods, above which the mountains suddenly present a most tremendous and precipitous front. On Crew green, far to the left, starts up Belin Mount, a round insulated rock remote from its congenial hills. See beneath me a vast extent of flat and wet country, the great plain of part of Shropshire.

Near a small brook, quit Trefaldwyn and enter the county of Salop or Shropshire. Visit, a little to the right, Wattleburg castle, an old house with a square tower of far more ancient date. It lies on the Roman road from Llanrhaeadr-ym-Mochnant. Mr William Mytton conjectures that the site might have been a station of a party of the Vandals sent into Britain by the emperor Probus and that the word is corrupted from Vandlesburgh, a name given it by the Saxons and derived, as is supposed, from the same cause.

On a lofty bank above the river at Little Shrawardine, saw a vast artificial mount, the former site of some castelet. From this place I descended to the Severn and, crossing the river, at this time fordable, I visited the castle and village of Great Shrawardine seated on the opposite bank. Only 3 or 4 fragments of the castle remain. It had never been considerable and was placed on a low mount destitute of outworks. The property of the castle, and the estates belonging to it, were of late years sold to Lord Clive.

The river, from the neighbourhood of Shrawardine, begins to grow very beautiful. The banks are elevated and often clothed with hanging woods. In places they recede from the verge of the channel and leave a verdant space of intervening meadow. In 1374, or the 48th of Edward III, Montford bridge was found to be out of repair which induced the king to grant it pontage or a toll for 3 years to effect the reparation.

Shrewsbury is 4 miles in almost direct line from this place but I preferred following the course of the river, tempted by the extreme beauty of the ride. My entrance into the town was through the North Gate which, for greater security, in reality consists of 2 gates at a small distance from one another with a round tower on each side.

The castle stands on an eminence on the left. Only one part with 2 rounders remains, and the walls of the north and eastern sides. The keep was on a large artificial mount which shows this fortress to have been of Saxon or Celtic origin, notwithstanding the foundation is ascribed to the great Earl of Shrewsbury, Roger de Montgomery. The inside is cleared from buildings, excepting one house. The whole castle-yard is a garden and the mount is at present admirable only for its beautiful view.

The town of Shrewsbury is seated within a peninsular with the ground finely sloping in most parts to the river. The castle was judiciously placed on a narrow isthmus 200 yards wide which connects it to the main land. Roger de Montgomery, on whom almost the whole county was bestowed by the Conqueror, besides 158 manors in other parts of the kingdom, made this his principal seat. In order to extend his fortifications, he demolished 41 houses for this part of the town at that period was very populous. No remittance was made to the owners, notwithstanding the greatness of their loss. The place continued in the possession of the 2 sons of Roger de Montgomery: Hugh, who was slain in Ynys Môn, and that monster of cruelty Robert de Belesme who, after various struggles, was at length obliged to surrender this place, his honours and all his mighty possessions into the hands of his sovereign Henry I. In our times it got into the hands of Pulteney Earl of Bath and is now in those of William Pulteney.

The first attempt towards the walls of this town was made by Robert de Belesme who, to defend it against the king's forces then marching towards him, drew a wall from each side of the castle across the isthmus to the water-side. One is still remaining and, as I am informed, terminated with a square tower. Both these walls are preserved in Speed's plan of the place. The town was not defended by wall still the year 1219 when Henry III strongly urged the inhabitants to consider some means of defence against an enemy. At first he made them a grant of various small tolls but at length, finding those insufficient, was obliged to assist them. The work went on so slowly that the walls were not completed in less than 32 years. The town was paved in the next reign by the assistance of certain customs granted for that purpose.

There are many historical evidences of the antiquity of the town. It had been for many ages the capital of Powys and the seat of the princes. Brochmail Ysgythrog, who lived about the year 607, is said to have had his palace on the spot where St Chad's church now stands. The Welsh called it Pengwern (*the Head of the Alder-groves*) and Y Mwythig (*The Delight, I suppose of our princes*). The period in which the town arose is not certainly known but it is supposed to have been on the ruin of the Roman Uriconium, the Vreken Ceaster of the Saxons, and the modern Wroxeter (a small village about 4 miles from hence upon the Severn where may be still seen a large fragment of the ancient wall).

In the time of Edward the Confessor, Scrobbes Byrig, as the Saxons called it, was a considerable place. At that period there were 252 houses and the burgesses paid 7 pounds 16 shillings 8 pence in excise. Whenever the king lay in the town, 12 of the chief inhabitants kept watch about his person; and if he came there to hunt, the better sort of burgesses rode armed as his guard and the sheriff sent 36 footmen for their support while the king was resident among them. When the king left the town, the sheriff sent 24 horses to Lenteurde to conduct him to the first stage in Staffordshire.

When the sheriff went against the Welsh, which he had frequent occasion of doing, it was customary to summon 36 men at Marseteley park to give their service for 8 days. Those who neglected to go forfeited 40 shillings.

The king had here 3 masters of the mint who, like the other coiners of the county, were obliged to pay him 20 shillings at the end of 15 days while the money was out of the mint and while it was current. The town paid in all 20 pounds yearly; the king had 2 thirds, the sheriff one. As soon as the Norman reign commenced, it paid its new earl 40 pounds.

The first charter extant (for that of Henry I is lost) was one in 1189 from Richard I. King John enlarged the charter in 1199, permitting the citizens to elect 2 substantial discreet persons of their body as bailiffs for the government of the town; and that the common-council might choose 4 others to determine all pleas of the crown in the corporation and to be a check on the bailiffs themselves.

This town sent members from the beginning. The right of voting rests in burgesses living in the town and paying to church and poor according to a resolution of the house in 1709; but in 1714 it was resolved that foreign burgesses had a right to vote.

There is in this town no manufacture considerable enough to merit mention but it draws very great profit from those of Trefaldwyn. This place is the chief mart for them. About 700,000 yards of Welsh webbs, a coarse kind of woollen cloth, are brought here annually to the Thursday market; and bought up and dressed (that is, the wool is raised on one side) by a set of people called shearmen. At this time only 40 are employed but in the time of Queen Elizabeth the trade was so great that not fewer than 600 maintained themselves by this occupation. The cloth is sent chiefly to America to clothe the Negroes, or to Flanders where it is used by the peasants.

Flannels, both coarse and fine, are brought every other Monday (except when fairs intervene) to Y Trallwng and are chiefly consumed in England to the amount of 700,000 or 800,000 yards. The Shrewsbury drapers go every market to Y Trallwng for the sake of this commerce.

The disposition of the streets in Shrewsbury is extremely irregular as is the case with all ancient towns not of Roman origin. The free-school stands near the castle and was founded by Edward VI in 1552. The building was originally of wood but in 1595 a beautiful and extensive edifice of stone arose in its place. This contains the school, houses for the masters, and a library filled with a valuable collection of books and several curiosities; among them are 3 large sepulchral stones discovered by ploughing at Wroxeter. One stone is inscribed to M. Petronius, standard-bearer to the 14th double legion or a legion in which 2 had been formed into one. As this legion never was in Britain, the learned Dr Ward guesses ('Philosophical Transactions' 49, part 1, 196) that Petronius only came for his health and died here.

Two bridges connect this peninsular with the country. The Welsh bridge is a very ancient structure of 6 arches with a very handsome gateway at one end. On each side is a round tower and over the entrance a statue of a prince in armour, generally supposed to be intended for Richard duke of York for beneath his feet is a rose-sprig, a device usual on the seals of that great prince. This was not the original site of the statue, it having been fixed here after it had been removed from another place in 1695. At the Welsh end of the bridge formerly stood another tower of great strength, calculated to repel the inroads of my countrymen.

On an eminence above Franwel, a suburb beyond the bridge, stands Millington's hospital, a handsome brick building founded in 1734 by the will of Mr James Millington of this town, draper. It maintains 12 poor housekeepers of Franwel (single persons) and a charity-school for 20 boys

*Old Welsh Bridge at Shrewsbury*

and 20 girls of the same district, if to be found there; and if not, to be taken out of the nearest part of the parish of St Chad, there to be instructed and fitted for trades suitable to their stations, to have prayers constantly read morning and evening on school-days (for which the chaplain is to have 20 pounds a year), and to be decently clothed twice a year. The poor housekeepers are to receive 3 pounds 10 shillings a year apiece, a load of coal and a new coat or gown annually. These poor people are, on vacancy, elected out of 10 others, properly qualified, who till their election are to receive likewise annually a new coat or gown apiece. The founder was a true churchman for all dissenters and all persons not truly orthodox are to be excluded.

The new bridge is on the side of the town and is a very handsome building of 7 arches. It was begun in 1769 and built by subscription under the direction of Mr Gwynn, architect, a native of Shrewsbury. This succeeded a very ancient and incommodious narrow bridge with the usual obstruction, a gateway. Not far from hence, on the side of the river, stood the great mitred abbey of St Peter and St Paul founded in 1083 by Roger Earl of Shrewsbury and his countess Adelissa. It was peopled by Benedictine monks from Scez in Normandy, who arrived hungry and naked. Among the after endowments, I smile at these good men receiving from Earl Hugh the tithe of all the venison in Shropshire except such which ranged in the woods of Wenlock. The founder died in 1094 and was interred here, as was his son Hugh, slain in Ynys Môn.

On a lofty bank is seated the orphan-house, a fine brick building with 13 windows in front and 2 small wings. It was begun in 1760 and designed to receive part of the foundlings from the great hospital in London. They were first to be put out to nurse in the neighbourhood and at a proper age to have been brought into the house and under proper masters and mistresses taught such arts as would make them useful members of society. On the decline of the capital hospital, this great building became useless and is at present no more than a place of confinement for prisoners of war.

In August 1485 the town made some show of resisting the passage of the Earl of Richmond, afterwards Henry VII, in his way to meet Richard III and gave him battle. It is affirmed that Henry brought with the army which landed in Wales that dreadful pestilence, the sweating sickness or Sudor Anglicanus, which for about 60 years after infested this kingdom at different periods. In many places it swept away a third of the people. It began with a sweat which never left the patient till it destroyed him or till he recovered. It always began with the affection of one part, the sense of hot vapour running through the whole limb. The crisis never exceeded

24 hours but death often ensued in 3 or 10.

I determined to conclude my tour by a journey to Caer Caradog, a post of the celebrated Celtic hero Caractacus (Caradog). I went over the new bridge, passing by Condover which was formerly owned by my eldest maternal uncle Richard Mytton of Halston by virtue of his marriage with Miss Owen, heiress of the place. Not far from Condover is Pitchford, the seat of Adam Ottley. Near the house is a most remarkable pond which flings up in hot weather a vast quantity of strong bitumen greatly resembling pitch which gives name to the place. It serves all the uses of that commodity and an oil most efficacious in many disorders has been for a considerable time past extracted from it.

Near the 8-mile stone from Shrewsbury I reached Longnor, the house of my respected old friend Joseph Plymley. It is seated in a pretty vale and commands a fine view of Caer Caradog and Lawley Hill. From Longnor I visited Caer Caradog. I fell accidentally on the steepest part after a ride of about 3 miles. At the end of a laborious clamber up a green and smooth ascent, now and then mixed with small fragments of lava, I reached the summit impeded a little by the first ditch and rampart in a place where (from the exceeding steepness) they seemed totally unnecessary. The entrance and approach are very conspicuous and may even at present be easily travelled on horseback. The area slopes upwards and ends in a peak.

Notwithstanding this place is styled Caer Caradog, it certainly was not that which was attacked by Ostorius and so admirably described by Tacitus:

"Hinc montibus arduis, et si qua clementer accedi poterunt modum valli faxa praestruit." (There were steep hills on one side and, on the easier slopes, a wall of piled stones.)

But it wants the following:

"Et praefluebat amnis vado incerto." (A river lacking easy crossings.)

The learned editor of Camden places it at Castle Ditches about 3 miles south of Clun on the left of the road to Trefyclo and gives, as I am informed, a faithful description of the trenches and ramparts. I never saw the place therefore am uncertain on what river it stood, the fords of which were such matter of difficulty. No such river is to be seen near the post I ascended; it therefore could not have been the spot on which our hero was defeated yet it is highly probable that it had been a post occupied by him and that it was named from that circumstance.

# Index of place names and personal names

THE LAND OF *Old* RENOWN

GEORGE BORROW IN WALES

DEWI ROBERTS

*Visitors' Delight*

An Anthology of Visitors'
Impressions of North Wales

Edited, with notes and an introduction
by
Dewi Roberts

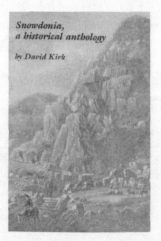

*Snowdonia,
a historical anthology*

*by David Kirk*

# Mountaineering & Botany

### The Complete Guide to Snowdon/Yr Wyddfa
– Robert Joes. PVC Cover; ISBN 0-86381-222-8; **£6.95**

### The Lakes of Eryri
– Geraint Roberts. Wildlife, fishing and folklore enhances this book aimed at anyone who loves Snowdonia. PVC cover; 256 pp; ISBN 0-86381-338-0; **£8.90**

### The Mountain Walker's Guide to Wales
– Colin Adams. A comprehensive guide to 100 routes covering 200 Welsh peaks. 192 pp; ISBN 0-86381-154-X; Map, PVC Cover; **£6.90**

### The Botanists and Guides of Snowdonia
– Dewi Jones. An account of the local guides and the plant hunters. 172 pp; ISBN 0-86381-383-6; **£6.95**

# Travellers in Wales

### Visitor's Delight
– Dewi Roberts. An anthology of visitor's impressions of North Wales. 152 pp; ISBN 0-86381-224-4; **£3.75**

### The A-Z of Betws-y-coed
– Donald Shaw. Full of facts, stories and history about the popular Welsh resort. 136 pp; 0-86381-153-1; **£2.99**

### Snowdonia, A Historical Anthology
– David Kirk. 60 writers portray the people and landscape of one of the most beautiful regions in Europe. 248 pp; ISBN 0-86381-270-8; **£5.95**

### All the Days were Glorious
– Gwyn Neale. George Gissing in North Wales – quotes from Gissing's letters and diary. 56 pp; ISBN 0-86381-286-4; **£2.95**

### The Land of Old Renown – George Borrow in Wales
– Dewi Roberts. A retrace of George Borrow's journey through Wales. ISBN 0-86381-436-0; **£4.50**

### Both Sides of the Border
An Anthology of writing on the Welsh Border Region by Dewi Roberts. ISBN 0-86381-461-1; **£4.75**

### A Tour in Wales by Thomas Pennant
An old classic abridged by David Kirk. 176 pp; ISBN 0-86381-473-5; **£5.75**

### Revd John Parker's Tour of Wales and its Churches (1798-160)
Abridged by Edgar W. Parry. ISBN 0-86381-481-6; **£4.75**

# Places & Poetry

### The Laugharne Poems
– Thomas Crowe. Poems by the first writer since Dylan Thomas to work from the boat house. ISBN 0-86381-432-8; **£4.50**

### Skywalls – A Snowdonia Sequence
Poems and Paintings by Clyde Holmes. ISBN 0-86381-466-2; **£5.75**

# Walks with History

*If you want to experience the very best of Wales, then these are the books for you. The walks are graded and there is something for everybody – short walks for families and more demanding routes to satisfy even the most experienced hillwalker.*
*Whether you choose to walk the high grounds, explore the beautiful valleys, study the varied wildlife or visit the remains of ancient castles and forts, the points of interest will explain what makes each area unique and help you choose the right walk for you.*

## Walks on the Llŷn Peninsula
PART 1 - SOUTH & WEST – N. Burras & J. Stiff.
ISBN 0-86381-343-7; **£4.50**
This series combines walks with history, stories and legends. Pastoral walks as well as coastal & mountain panoramas.

## Walks on the Llŷn Peninsula
PART 2 - NORTH & EAST – N. Burras & J. Stiff.
ISBN 0-86381-365-8; **£4.50**

## Walks in the Snowdonia Mountains
– Don Hinson. 45 walks, mostly circular, 96 pages, inc. accurate maps and drawings. 96pp ISBN 0-86381-385-2; New Edition: **£3.75**

## Walks in North Snowdonia
– Don Hinson. 100km of paths to help those wishing to explore the area further.
96pp ISBN 0-86381-386-0; New Edition; **£3.75**

## New Walks in Snowdonia
– Don Hinson. 43 circular walks together with many variations. This book introduces you to lesser known paths and places which guide book writers seem to have neglected. Maps with every walk. Pen & ink drawings.
96pp ISBN 0-86381-390-9; New Edition; **£3.75**

## Circular Walks in North Pembrokeshire
– Paul Williams, 14 walks, 112 pages. ISBN 0-86381-420-4; **£4.50**

## Circular Walks in South Pembrokeshire
– Paul Williams, 14 walks, 120 pages. ISBN 0-86381-421-2; **£4.50**

## From Mountain Tops to Valley Floors
Salter & Worral. ISBN 0-86381-430-1; **£4.50**
Detailed information for casual/family walks and for the more adventurous walker.

## NEW FOR 1998:
### Circular Walks in the Brecon Beacons National Park;
ISBN 0-86381-476-X; **£4.50**
### Circular Walks on Anglesey; ISBN 0-86381-478-6; **£4.50**
### Circular Walks in Gower; ISBN 0-86381-479-4; **£4.50**
### Circular Walks in Central Wales; ISBN 0-86381-480-8; **£4.50**
### Circular Walks in Gwent; ISBN 0-86381-477-8; **£4.50**

### Supernatural Clwyd
– Richard Holland. A collection of Clwyd's supernatural folktales. 210 pp; many illustrations and photographs; ISBN 0-86381-127-2; **£4.50**

### Haunted Clwyd
– Richard Holland. From Clwyd's rich heritage of folklore to present day first-hand accounts, here are phantoms of all descriptions, homely or terrifying. 144 pp; many illustrations; ISBN 0-86381-218-X; **£3.50**

### Bye-Gones
– Richard Holland. Old volumes of Bye-Gones, a periodical published between 1871 and 1939, are a treasure trove of anecdotes relating to Wales and the Border Counties. Black & white illustrations. 120pp; ISBN 0-86381-239-2; **£3.50**

### When the Devil Roamed Wales
– Jane Pugh. An insight into days gone by when Wales was riddled with satanic legends and stories. Including cartoons. 120 pp; ISBN 0-86381-087-X; **£2.50**

### Welsh Ghostly Encounters
– Jane Pugh. A collection of ancient stories and also a few recent accounts of ghostly encounters. 136 pp; ISBN 0-86381-152-3; **£2.75**

### Ways with Hazel and Horn
– Bob Griff/Meurig Owen. Traditional stickmaking. ISBN 0-86381-367-4; **£3.95**

### Rumours and Oddities from North Wales
A selection of folklore, myths & ghost stories – Meirion Hughes and Wayne Evans. A fascinating collection of stories, presenting legends, folk heroes and sinister ghosts. New edition. Many illustrations. 112 pp; ISBN 0-86381-337-2; **£3.00**

### The Haunting of Glamorgan and Gwent
– Russell Gascoigne. This book records numerous examples of other worldly phenomena – tales of shipwrecks, pirates and smugglers, of haunted castles, crumbling ruins and remote farmhouses. Many illustrations. 104 pp; ISBN 0-86381-262-7; **£3.75**

### Tales of Old Glamorgan
– Wendy Hughes. In this book, Wendy Hughes brings alive the tales which lie at the heart of the county of Glamorgan – legends, fables of fairies and magic, as well as stories of devils, witches and ghosts. Black and white illustrations. 132 pp; ISBN 0-86381-287-2; **£4.25**

### Gods and Heroes in North Wales – A Mythological Guide
– Michael Senior. Here, the author deals with the true mythology of Britain, some important parts of which are located in North Wales. Black and white illustrations. 96 pp; ISBN 0-86381-249-X; £3.25

### Country Churchyards in Wales
– Donald Gregory. Including maps and illustrations. ISBN 0-86381-183-3; **£3.50**

### Celtic High Crosses of Wales
– John Sharkey. ISBN 0-86381-489-1; **£5.75**

**SUPERNATURAL CLWYD**
The Folk Tales of North-East Wales

Richard Holland

**WAYS WITH HAZEL AND HORN**
BOB GRIFF JONES
and MEURIG OWEN

*Gods and Heroes*
IN NORTH WALES
*A Mythological Guide*

Michael Senior